SO GREAT SALVATION

The Meaning and Message of the Letter to the Hebrews

THE LETTER TO THE HEBREWS BOTH attracts and baffles the reader. It clearly deals with most important topics, but it does so in a style that seems too remote for us to understand. Yet in fact it could hardly be more relevant to any period of Christian history than to ours. It is a Letter of tension – tension between faith and unbelief, between holding on and letting go, between moving forward and slipping back. These same tensions characterize the times in which we live and for this reason it has an urgent and relevant message to us all.

In this book the author, former Vice-Principal of Oak Hill College, London, makes it clear that the central challenge of "Hebrews" is as fresh today as ever. He shows that the main purpose of the Epistle is to lead us to a spiritually mature Christian life, characterized by positive devotion to Christ and a sober, serious determination, by His help, to run the race and attain the goal.

D1099606

OTHER TITLES IN THIS SERIES:

SO
GREAT
SALVATION

The Meaning and Message of the Letter to the Hebrews

Alan M. Stibbs, M.A.

THE PATERNOSTER PRESS

ISBN: 0 85364 102 1

AUSTRALIA:
Emu Book Agencies Pty., Ltd.,
511 Kent Street, Sydney, N.S.W.

CANADA:
Home Evangel Books Ltd.,
25 Hobson Avenue, Toronto, 16

SOUTH AFRICA:
Oxford University Press,
P.O. Box 1141, Thibault House,
Thibault Square, Cape Town

Made and Printed in Great Britain for
The Paternoster Press Paternoster House
3 Mount Radford Crescent Exeter Devon
by Cox & Wyman Limited Fakenham

Contents

Preface

IT IS FORTY YEARS AGO THAT I FIRST BEGAN A SERIOUS DETAILED study of the Epistle to the Hebrews. Over the years, both in private study and in public ministry, I have on very many occasions found its exposition a most absorbing and satisfying interest. In writing these studies of its themes I have once again enjoyed a God-given feast of good things, in which I hope this book may in some small measure help others to share.

I am indebted to many who by their writings have helped me to appreciate more of the wealth of truth which this Epistle contains. I ought in particular to mention the commentaries of B. F. Westcott, A. B. Davidson and F. Delitzsch; also *The Holiest of All* by Andrew Murray, *Let us go on* by W. H. Griffith Thomas, and *The Letter to the Hebrews* by William Barclay.

Except where otherwise indicated, the quotations of Scripture are taken from the Revised Standard Version.

ALAN M. STIBBS

One

The Epistle as a Whole

Its Author

SINCE THE THIRD CENTURY A.D. THIS EPISTLE HAS BEEN KNOWN AS the Epistle of Paul to the Hebrews. The text of the epistle, however, does not indicate either who wrote it, or to whom it was written. Nor do we intend here critically to discuss such questions. They have been dealt with by the present writer in a contribution to *The New Bible Commentary, Revised*.[1] A fuller treatment of them may be found in Dr. Donald Guthrie's *New Testament Introduction: Hebrews to Revelation*.[2] For our present purpose we shall accept the epistle as God's Word to us. In other words, we believe that God Himself is the primary author and Christians of every age are the divinely intended readers. *Therefore, as the Holy Spirit says, Today, when you hear his voice, do not harden your hearts.*[3] *See that you do not refuse him who is speaking.*[4] Rather prepare yourself as you read to hear God's Word; to heed it, to believe it, and to obey it.

The Readers' Condition

From the epistle we can learn much about the readers' spiritual condition. It is this which explains why the writer wrote as he did. So some appreciation of this is essential to proper understanding.

These Christians were showing unhealthy signs of failure in midcourse. Unquestionably they had made a good beginning in their initial response to Christ and the gospel.[5] But they had all too obviously lost their first love. They had become "slothful" or "sluggish"[6] in their response. They were no longer quick to act in

---

[1] I.V.F., 1970, pp. 1191–94.
[2] Tyndale Press, 1962, pp. 11–59.
[3] 3:7, 8.   [4] 12:25.
[5] See 10:32–34.
[6] 5:11, "dull"; 6:12.

the light of the God-given word. Their latent spiritual powers were undeveloped. They were visibly immature; incapable of proper grown-up participation in Christian thought and practice; feeding on milk, not solid food.[7] They were showing signs of becoming weary and faint-hearted,[8] and of ceasing to go on. Consequently they were in danger of failing to inherit the promises given to them in Christ.[9] What was worse, they were in danger of being misled by diverse and strange teachings,[10] of drifting away from what they had heard,[11] and even of becoming apostate and completely abandoning faith in Christ.[12] If this last possibility happened it would expose them to God's terrifying judgment.

It is, too, very relevant to recognize that, as former adherents of Judaism, they may well have become deeply disappointed with Christianity. For it had not fulfilled their Jewish expectations. Christ had not reappeared to establish His promised kingdom. The vast majority of their fellow-Jews had decisively rejected the claims of Jesus to be the promised Messiah; so perhaps it was those who had believed in Him who were in the wrong. In addition, continued confession of Jesus as the Christ was openly involving them in increasing reproach and, possibly before long, in violent persecution. They may well therefore have been tempted to go back on their Christian confession and to return to Judaism as clearly preferable.

The Writer's Concern

Knowing that those who were to read his letter were in such an unsatisfactory condition, this writer is concerned to awaken them to a full awareness of the high possibilities and the awful perils between which they are half-heartedly hesitating. His chosen method of appealing to them is to use in turn reasoned exposition, challenging exhortation, forbidding warning. By repeated use of the Old Testament Scriptures, whose divine origin and authority they fully recognize, he sets himself to demonstrate the superiority of Christ and of the new covenant over the prophets, angels, leaders and high priests whom God used under the old order. He shows that Christ brings fulfilment which is heavenly, and perfection which is

---

[7] 5:12-14.
[8] 12:3, 12.
[9] See 4:1; 6:12; 10:35, 36.
[10] 13:9.
[11] 2:1.
[12] 3:12; 10:26-29.

eternal. He indicates that these necessarily supersede what were only shadows of the good things to come. Christ, he says, "abolishes the first in order to establish the second".[13]

He also warns them that, if their unsatisfactory present condition is not soon made better, it could easily become radically, if not fatally, worse. He tells them repeatedly that for the full possession of all that God has promised steadfast endurance is required; having begun to believe they must keep on believing. So he urges them to clear the road for advance, to stir themselves to fresh effort, to strive to enter in. In order to ensure the full maintenance of active faith and obedience he exhorts them in intimate personal fellowship daily to encourage one another; and he explicitly enjoins them not to fail to meet regularly together with such mutual encouragement in view. Just as their love is zealous in "serving the saints", so, he says, "we desire each one of you to show the same earnestness in realizing the full assurance of hope until the end".[14]

The Epistle's Relevance Today

It is not difficult to see that such an epistle has an abiding value and a continuing message. Words written by Andrew Murray in 1894 with reference to this epistle can be aptly quoted as if written today.

> It is as if nothing could be written more exactly suited to the state of the whole Church of Christ in the present day. The great complaint of all who have the care of souls is the lack of whole-heartedness, of steadfastness, of perseverance and progress in the Christian life. Many, of whom one cannot but hope that they are true Christians, come to a standstill, and do not advance beyond the rudiments of Christian life and practice. And many more do not even remain stationary, but turn back to a life of worldliness, of formality, of indifference. And the question is continually being asked – what is the want in our religion that, in so many cases, it gives no power to stand, to advance, to press on unto perfection? And what is the teaching that is needed to give that health and vigour to the Christian life that, through all adverse circumstances, it may be able to hold fast the beginning firm to the end? The teaching of this epistle is the divine answer to these questions.[15]

[13] 10:9.   [14] 6:10–12.
[15] *The Holiest of All*; p. 5, 6.

So in confronting present-day readers with its challenge one does not merely have to say, "Long ago, as the Spirit once said", but *as the Holy Spirit says, Today, when you hear his voice, do not harden your hearts.*[16]

[16] 3:7, 8.

Two

God's Full and Final Word to Men

I : I–4

THE WEALTH OF THOUGHT IN THESE OPENING VERSES DEFIES adequate exposition. It is appropriate, too, that such wealth should be impressively expressed. "This is," writes Dr. William Barclay of these verses, "the most sonorous piece of Greek in the whole New Testament. It is a passage that any classical Greek orator would have been proud to write. The writer of the Letter to the Hebrews has brought to it every artifice of word and rhythm that the beautiful and flexible Greek language could provide." He "felt that, since he was going to speak of the supreme revelation of God to men, he must clothe his thought in the noblest language that it was possible to find".[1]

God Has Spoken to Us

Two truths are taken for granted; one that God is, and the other that He is able to make Himself known to men. But much more than that is here. For what is possible is here declared to have happened. The mighty sovereign Creator God has declared Himself in personal action. He has revealed not only His mind but also Himself. He offers us in Christ not only fuller knowledge of His ways, but also personal participation in the fulfilment of His eternal purposes. Because God has so spoken we are, or can become, *heirs of salvation.*[2] No wonder the writer says, therefore, that we ought to pay heed.[3] No wonder he chooses in opening his letter to confront his readers not with himself as the writer, but with God as the speaker and with Christ as the living Word from God. So our answer must be given to Him. God Himself is the one "with whom we have to do".[4] Answerable we are, and answer we must; for God has spoken to us.

[1] *The Letter to the Hebrews,* p. I.
[2] I : I4, AV.
[3] See 2 : I.
[4] See 4 : I3.

God Incarnate

God's full and final word to men is spoken in Christ – in His person and work. It finds expression in One who is God's *Son*, sharing God's nature; and so Himself the key to Deity.[5] It finds expression, also, in One who is the appointed *heir of all things*; and so Himself the key to the universe.[6]

God makes Himself fully known, first, in Christ's person; that is, in what Christ is. For He is Himself God, the actual outshining of God's glory, and the exact expression of God's nature. He is rightly confessed in an ancient creed as "God of God, Light of Light, Very God of Very God". In other words, because of His divine origin, He is Himself one hundred per cent GOD.[7]

In the second place, God makes Himself fully known in what Christ does. The created order is itself an evidence of His working.[8] For by His Son God created the world. By His own word of power the Son of God upholds the universe. And all things are made for His possession as their appointed heir. He is therefore their author, sustainer and Lord.

But God is supremely and finally revealed to men in what Christ has done as man on earth; that is, in His work of redemption by which He made *purification for sins*. This involved incarnation and sacrifice. This was crowned by exaltation to possess the appointed inheritance; which He did not only as God the Son, but also as being now Himself the glorified and triumphant Man.

Two Complementary Movements

The passage records two movements, one of revelation and one of reconciliation, movements which significantly reach their complete fulfilment together. Because of the defilement and damage wrought by sin, God could not make Himself fully known to men except by acting for their rescue and redemption. Since God is love, He could not express Himself manwards without intervening to save. So the act of God by which God is completely revealed to men itself provides a reconciliation of men to God. Or, putting the same truths the other way round, we may say that the action of God for men's benefit, by which man is fully reconciled to God, is itself a final

[5] Cf. Jn., 14:9.   [6] Cf. Eph., 1:9, 10.
[7] Cf. Col. 1:19; 2:9.   [8] See Ps., 19:1.

revelation to men of the character and will of God.[9] We know what God is like from what He has done for us.

The participation of the Son of God in these two movements is implied by the description of Him in chapter three as our *apostle and high priest*.[10] For apostles are sent forth from God as messengers of revelation to men; and it is the work of a high priest as man to represent men, and by the offering of sacrifice for sin to achieve reconciliation to God.

Twice in the Greek of this passage an introductory participial clause is followed by a main finite verb. First we read that God "having spoken . . . spoke". Later we read of the Son that He "having made purification for sins sat down". The first of these statements clearly concerns revelation, that is, the activity by which God has made Himself known to men. The second statement equally obviously concerns reconciliation, that is, the activity by which God puts men right with Himself. In each case the phraseology indicates that an initiating activity found its consummation; the first in decisive completion and the second in permanent consequence. Let us now consider more closely the character and content of these two movements.

A Perfect and Final Revelation

God "having spoken . . . spoke". The phraseology emphasizes that God has spoken in two complementary ways, the first subordinate and preparatory, the second final and consummatory. The revelation given in the Old Testament is thus characterized as partial and varied, introductory and incomplete; but not, on that account, at any point inaccurate. It was given fragmentarily, here a little and there a little. Thus it was capable of being all fitted together into a coherent whole only in the light of its subsequent fulfilment. It was essentially forward-looking, awaiting completion for full explanation. Consequently, as Augustine said, what was in the Old Testament enfolded is in the New Testament unfolded.

God also spoke by many methods, in law and prophecy, in promise and warning, in type and allegory, by dreams and visions, by judgments and deliverances. God spoke, too "in the prophets",[11]

[9] Cf., I Jn., 4:9, 10.
[10] 3:1.
[11] See I:I, RV.

and not just by them. They were not just messengers or mouth-
pieces of words external to themselves. The whole man and his
particular historical environment, his individual personality and his
actual experiences, were all made to contribute to the utterance of
God's word.

In Christ and by His coming God's utterance has now been completed. We live in the days of fulfilment or consummation. The
word given by God to men in His incarnate Son is perfect, final and
eternal. It cannot be added to or superseded. God Himself, so to
speak, has nothing more to say.

In illustration of this characteristic of finality we may compare
the words about the owner of the vineyard in the parable about the
wicked husbandmen. "He had yet one beloved son: he sent him
last unto them."[12] When the husbandmen rejected him and killed
him, there was nothing else possible or appropriate but judgment.
The writer of the epistle is similarly aware that such a crowning
revelation as God has given of Himself to men in Christ confronts us
either with our supreme opportunity to embrace the best, or, if we
reject Him, the direst peril of being involved in the worst. *How*, he
asks, *shall we escape, if we neglect such a great salvation?*[13]

A Full and Permanent Reconciliation

The earthly work of the incarnate Son of God and the whole purpose of His becoming Man found their immediate completion, and
realized their chief intention, in His death. So, in the brief summary
statements with which this epistle begins, this is the one earthly
activity which is mentioned; that He *made purification for sins*. By
the sacrifice of Himself He actually achieved what the Old Testament ritual ceremonies had only figuratively anticipated; that is, the
actual cleansing of sin's defilement which is later described as the
putting away of sin.[14]

The success and the significance of this achievement are then
indicated by the declaration of its permanent heavenly consequence.
He sat down at the right hand of the Majesty on high. He was
enthroned by God Himself, and given by God the assurance of complete triumph over every foe. For to Him God said *"Sit at my right
hand, till I make thy enemies a stool for thy feet."*[15]

[12] Mk., 12:6, RV.   [13] 2:3.
[14] See 7:27; 9:26.   [15] 1:13; cf., 10:11–13.

It is here important for us to realize with wonder that Jesus was thus enthroned by God as the triumphant Man, as our high priest. What we can now see is the human *Jesus crowned with glory and honour*.[16] "The chief point," says the writer of this Epistle, in what he is here striving to say is that we have as our high priest one who is seated "on the right hand of the throne of the Majesty in the heavens."[17] We are the people who are intended to appropriate and to enjoy the consequently available benefits.

For Christ's entrance, acceptance and enthronement in God's presence *on our behalf*[18] makes it possible for us to come boldly into the very sanctuary of God's presence.[19] We are no longer, because of sin, either abhorrent in God's sight or shut out from His presence. Reconciliation to God is thus fully obtained for us; and we are invited from now on continuously to enjoy the available benefits by ourselves drawing near to God through Christ in order to appropriate them.

The Consummation of God's Purpose and of Man's Destiny

On the one hand, this enthronement of Christ as King of the universe fulfils God's eternal purpose for His Son. For in eternity, before the universe was created, God appointed Him as the heir who was to possess it as His own inheritance. Here we see this purpose being realized and its final completion divinely assured. *For*, as St. Paul says elsewhere, *He must reign until he has put all his enemies under his feet*.[20]

On the other hand, this exaltation from the grave to the throne of Jesus the Man means also nothing less than the fulfilment in Him of man's divinely intended destiny. For man at his creation was told that he was to have dominion.[21] The inspired psalmist had spoken of him as *crowned* by God *with glory and honour*, with everything put in subjection under his feet.[22] And here we see this lordship over the world given to Jesus, the Man. He is *crowned with glory and honour*.[23] So in Him man's destiny is already realized.

---

[16] 2:9. [17] 8:1, RV.
[18] See 6:20; 9:24. [19] See 4:16; 10:19–22
[20] 1 Cor., 15:25.
[21] See Gen., 1:28.
[22] See 2:7, 8 quoted from Ps. 8:5, 6.
[23] 2:9.

B

Our Prophet, Priest and King

Consequently the full embrace of the fulfilment achieved in Christ, through the incarnation, death and exaltation of God's Son, is threefold. In Him God spoke His final word of revelation. By His own act and sacrifice He made propitiation for sin and finished the work of reconciliation. Then He sat down on the throne whence He now reigns. So He is our prophet, priest and king. And, as the writer of this Epistle goes on to make unmistakably plain, it was through what happened at the Cross that revelation was completed, that reconciliation was achieved, and that a new triumphant reign began.

Three

The Pioneer of Our Salvation

1:5–14; 2:5–3:6

THE PRACTICAL INTEREST FOR US OF THIS WHOLE PASSAGE IS
that it concerns God's provision for us of *a great salvation*.[1] Of
this salvation we are chosen to be the "heirs"[2] and Christ was
appointed to be *the pioneer*.[3] The two truths which are here chiefly
to occupy our attention are the greatness of the person who has
thus become our Saviour, and the character of the work in which
He engaged to procure this salvation for us. This salvation is the
more outstanding, because it means nothing less than the realization
by man of his divinely intended destiny; and because it means
man's participation in a fulfilment, which is not private and indi-
vidualistic, but one to be fully enjoyed only in the company of
God's people. For we may find here, first, the evidence of man's
entrance into his true glory; and second, the accompanying emergence of the redeemed community – the *many sons* who together
constitute the family or the church of God.[4]

Greater than Angels: A Double Superiority: 1:4–14

Jesus, the Son of God, who is to be the central object of our interest
in this whole epistle, is here declared to be greater than angels in
two ways; first, as being Himself God, the eternal Son of the Father,
and second, through becoming the glorified and exalted Man. The
initial emphasis is on the first truth, and the ultimate emphasis is on
the second. Throughout, the writer of the epistle has both truths in
mind. Some of the Scriptures which he quotes and the statements
which he makes seem – perhaps deliberately – capable of referring
to either or to both.

The name "Son" unmistakably refers, in the first place, as we
have seen, to Christ's deity as "very God of very God". But, in the
second place, it is *the name He has obtained*,[5] or the status which

[1] 2:3.
[2] 1:14, AV.
[3] 2:10.
[4] See 2:10–12.
[5] 1:4.

He has acquired, as the exalted Man. The writer quotes God's words, *"Thou art my Son, today I have begotten thee."*[6] Christ is here addressed as One who is already God's Son, and yet as One who has "today" been begotten into the status of sonship. This same Scripture is quoted by Paul with reference to the resurrection of Jesus from the dead;[7] for that was the day when it was fulfilled. Also, the same fuller truth of fresh adoption into a permanent status is expressed in the following quotation: *"I will be to him a father, and he shall be to me a son."*[8] So, as Man, Christ has *become as much superior to the angels as the name he has obtained is more excellent than theirs.*[9]

Similarly the term *the firstborn* can be a reference to Christ's deity as begotten of God, and as Himself the heir or lord of all creation.[10] But, it can also refer to His entrance as Man into the glory of resurrection as *the firstborn from the dead*, and the beginning and head of the church.[11] The whole of verse 6 is also capable of a double reference. It can refer to Christ's first advent, meaning that, when God brought His Son into the world at the incarnation, the angels acknowledged His deity in worship. The statement, can, however, be taken, as some responsible expositors have taken it, to refer to Christ's second advent, when God will again bring Him into the inhabited earth;[12] and then, though He comes visibly as the glorified Man, the firstborn from the dead, He will also be hailed and worshipped by the angels as God coming to judge the earth.[13]

So, from first to last, first as from all eternity Himself God, and finally as now and henceforth the exalted Man, Jesus, the Son of God, is superior to the angels. For they are but creatures of God, and *ministering spirits sent forth to serve*[14] men.

His Deity as God the Son: 1 : 5–12

By some of the Scriptures here quoted the deity of Christ is either explicitly indicated or unmistakably implied. By God's own command He is to be given by all God's angels the worship which is

[6] 1 : 5.   [7] See Acts 13 : 33.
[8] From 2 Sam. 7 : 14.   [9] 1 : 4.
[10] See Col. 1 : 15.   [11] See Col. 1 : 18; cf. Rev. 1 : 5.
[12] See 1 : 6, RV and mg.
[13] See Ps. 97; 7 and Dt. 32 : 43 from Gk. of which this may be cited.
[14] 1 : 14.

due – worship which can only rightly be given to God alone.[15] In contrast to the ministerial and creaturely offices of the angels, He occupies for ever the throne as God, and enjoys a unique anointing of God's Spirit.[16]

As God He existed before the universe was made. As God He will endure eternally unchanged after the universe has passed away. Indeed, as its Creator and Lord, He laid its foundation in its beginning, and at its end He will put it on one side like a used and worn-out garment. But He Himself abides eternally the same.[17] It is His deity that constitutes Him the mediator of a full and final revelation, which must surpass and supersede any revelation given by angels. This is why *we must pay the closer attention to what we have heard*, because it has been spoken not merely by angels but *by the Lord* Himself.[18]

His Humanity as Jesus: 2:9–18

The writer of this epistle particularly stresses the truth that Jesus has become greater than angels as the exalted Man. He explicitly indicates the direction of his interest by calling our Lord by His human name *Jesus*[19] – without the usual addition of other descriptive titles, such as Lord or Christ.

This emphasis on our Lord's humanity also particularly concerns our salvation, because of the realization in Jesus as Man and for our benefit of man's intended destiny. As we have previously noticed, the day of the resurrection of Jesus was the day when as Man He was begotten to a new status in God's sight. He thus became superior to the angels as the representative Man, and as the mediator of salvation to men. His glorification as Man is the pattern as well as the pledge of our own entrance as God's sons into glory. Also, as other New Testament writers equally emphasize, it was when Jesus through His resurrection was exalted as Man into heaven, and given His seat at the right hand of God, that *angels, authorities and powers* were made *subject to him*.[20] The person whose achievements we are here invited to consider is One who Himself partook of human nature – of flesh and blood like ours[21] – and who has

---

[15] 1:6.   [16] See 1:7–9.
[17] See 1:10–12.   [18] 2:1–4.
[19] See 2:9; 3:1; 6:20; 12:2, 24; 13:12.
[20] See 1 Pet. 3:22; cf. Eph. 1:19–22.
[21] See 2:14.

been enthroned as Man at God's right hand. The One, therefore, whom we may now see crowned with glory and honour, the One to whom we are to look for inspiration, and to whom we are to come for help, is *Jesus*[22] – the Man.

God's Purpose for Man: 2:5-10

God's revealed purpose, as Scripture explicitly indicates, is that men and not angels are the divinely predestinated lords of the created order. For instance, in Psalm 8 it is made plain that, although man begins in this present world-order by being made *for a little while lower than the angels*, God's ultimate purpose for man is to crown him with glory and honour, and to put *everything in subjection under his feet*[23] – including the angels.[24] The angels are simply ministering spirits, commissioned by God to further these ends; *sent forth*, that is, *to serve, for the sake of those* (i.e. men) *who are to obtain salvation*.[25]

Clearly, also, as the writer of this epistle immediately acknowledges, this intended consummation is not yet fully realized. We do not at present see man where he ought to be, and where God intends him to be, as lord of creation with everything in subjection to him.[26] Fulfilment must, therefore, still be spoken of as future. So the writer is careful to add that it is *the world to come, of which we are speaking;*[27] that is, things as they will be when God's purpose for men is fully completed. Meanwhile, what we do see is Jesus, the Man, possessing the condition of glory, and occupying the position of dominion, which are intended for men; that is, He is crowned with glory and honour, with everything put, or to be put, in subjection under His feet.[28]

Here, in Jesus exalted in glory at God's right hand, faith may see the outwrought fulfilment of man's true destiny. It is God's purpose for men that is here seen to be both realized and realizable. For Jesus reached this goal not for His own exclusive enjoyment but as *the pioneer*[29] of our salvation – as *a forerunner*[30] whom we may follow. No matter, therefore, how bad things may sometimes look at the moment, God's purposes for man have not failed. We may live in hope.

[22] See 2:9; 12:2, 24.
[23] 2:6–8; from Ps. 8:4–6.
[24] See 1 Cor. 6:3.
[25] 1:14.
[26] 2:8c.
[27] 2:5.
[28] 2:9; 1:13; 10:12, 13.
[29] 2:10.
[30] 6:20.

The Way of Fulfilment – Through Jesus: 2:5–18

What the writer of this epistle is perhaps most concerned to explain is the character of God's chosen way to this fulfilment of man's destiny. He is eager to make his readers aware of its complete suitability, its staggering cost and its amazing consequences. It explains why the eternal Son of God became as Man for a little while lower than the angels, and was beset with weakness and subject to temptation.[31] It explains also why He descended still lower into humiliation, suffering and shame in order on behalf of all other men to *taste death*; that is, fully to experience and exhaust the awful character of death as the consequence of sin.

What God thus chose to do in Christ was determined both by man's need, and by God's purpose. For far from entering into his intended dominion over creation man had become a slave of things created. He was defiled by sin. He was a helpless victim, held in bondage by the power of death and the devil. What he needed was salvation. He needed a priest to make propitiation for his sins. He needed a deliverer to destroy for him the power of death and of the devil. He needed help to face the inevitable temptations experienced during life in this world. In addition to all this, God's full purpose for man was not only to rescue him from these hostile powers, but also still to fulfil His original intention as man's Creator, and to bring men to glory to enjoy the status and privileges of sons of God.

In order to meet such needs and to further such ends it was divinely fitting – it was morally congruous with the character of God Himself, and with the way in which as sovereign Creator and Lord He does things – to effect men's full salvation by providing a suffering pioneer.[32]

So the eternal Son of God appeared in history on earth as Jesus the Man. He came into the midst of the human situation as it was, in order from inside to open up a way out of it; and in order, as a pioneer, to provide for men a way of escape from bondage and death, a way of access into God's presence, and a way of entrance into man's intended glory.

This could be done only if the Son of God not only Himself became truly Man, but also if in His own human body of flesh and blood He triumphed over sin and the devil by submitting to

[31] See 2:9, 18; 4:15; 5:2, 7.
[32] 2:10.

suffering and death. This is the cost which He faced; and this is why He faced it. He *for a little while was made lower than the angels . . . so that by the grace of God he might taste death for every one.*[33] Because those whom God would own as His children *share in flesh and blood, he himself likewise partook of the same nature, that through death he might destroy him who has the power of death, that is the devil.*[34] For *he had to be made like his brethren in every respect*[35] if He was to help them; and those whom He was not ashamed thus to own as brethren were not angels but men – and, more particularly, the descendants of Abraham.[36]

So He chose to become Man, and as Man to suffer temptation and death. Only so could He become the kind of high priest who could make propitiation for men's sins, and help men when they are tempted.[37] All this He chose to do, and did. Thus as the pioneer of men's salvation He was made *perfect;*[38] that is, He fully accomplished in outworked achievement all that was necessary to make it possible for Him henceforth to function as man's all-sufficient Saviour.

The consequences of His saving work are, therefore, amazing; and, what is more, they are actually available to be enjoyed by you and me. They are explicitly demonstrated as already achieved by His own exaltation as Man to the right hand of God. *Because of the suffering of death, He was crowned with glory and honour.*[39] From the seat of His triumph and God-given reward He is able to provide a full and complete salvation for all who make Him their confidence, and come to God by the way out of sin and the way into the sanctuary which He has opened for us.[40]

Jesus Greater Than Moses: 3 : 1–6

In Jewish eyes, and according to the Old Testament Scriptures, Moses held a unique place in God's dealings with men. He was the man with whom God spoke face to face and not, as to the prophets in general, in dreams and visions. He was in a special way entrusted

[33] 2 : 9.   [34] 2 : 14.
[35] 2 : 17.   [36] See 2 : 11, 16.
[37] 2 : 17, 18.   [38] 2 : 10.
[39] 2 : 9.   [40] 7 : 25; 10 : 19–22.

by God with the care of all His people.[41] He led them forth from bondage into salvation. At Sinai he was the mediator of God's covenant with them. So Israelites traced back to Moses their sense of calling and status as the consecrated people of God.

Jesus is now to be confessed and followed as similar to, but greater than, Moses. He, too, has been divinely appointed, and has proved faithful in the discharge of His appointed work. It is through Him that as "holy brethren" we are called and consecrated to be God's people or house.[42]

Yet Christ is also worthy of more honour than Moses because[43] He is not, like Moses, merely a servant, and himself a member of the house. For, as God, He is both the builder and the lord of the house. Because He is God's Son, the house is His own. Moses as a figure anticipated a later fulfilment. He pointed forward to that which should come after. Christ is Himself, in His own person and work, the final reality, the fulfilment of all that Moses fore-shadowed. He points to none but Himself. *Therefore, holy brethren, who share a heavenly call, consider Jesus.*[44] For full salvation be-comes ours wholly through Him.

We Are His House[45]

This purpose of God for men and above all for His Son, and this appointed work of Christ for our salvation, alike find their fulfil-ment in the emergence of a redeemed community. Christ's concern as a faithful high priest was to make propitiation for the sins of the people,[46] and to consecrate the many as "holy brethren" to be one with Him as sons or children of God.[47] So He is not ashamed to own us as His brethren. There is here a significant quotation from Psalm 22, a psalm which speaks prophetically first of Christ's shameful suffering, and then of His triumph and consequent praise to God in the midst of the "church" (Gk *ecclesia*) or *congregation* gathered to give God worship.[48] For, once we belong by the grace of God to this company, Christ is pleased to manifest His presence in our midst, and to say of us in witness: *"Here am I and the children God has given me."*[49] In other words, we are thus privileged in

[41] See Num. 12:5–8.
[43] See 3:3–6.
[45] 3:6.
[47] 2:11; 3:1.
[49] 2:13.
[42] 3:1, 2.
[44] 3:1.
[46] 2:17.
[48] 2:12 from Ps. 22:22.

consequence of His saving work to belong to His house or church. But this participation will be fully ours only if, steadfastly to the end, we hold fast to our confidence in Christ and to the outspoken confession of our faith in Him.[50] This is why, as we shall next go on to consider, exhortation both to take heed and to draw near are so pertinent.

[50] See 3:6, 14.

Four

The Demand for Our Response

2 : 1–4; 3 : 7–4 : 13

THIS EPISTLE IS, BY ITS WRITER'S OWN DESCRIPTION, PRIMARILY A *word of exhortation*.[1] He was eager to stir his readers to fuller response towards Christ and the gospel. While he does devote big sections of the epistle to doctrinal exposition, he introduces these to give substance to his appeals and to provide solid foundation on which to base his words of more practical challenge. What he wrote, therefore, continues to achieve the end which he had in view only when it is used of God to make readers think and act differently. Consequently all who would seriously and profitably pursue this study further must prepare themselves to be personally challenged by solemn warnings and urgent, imperative exhortations. They must seek for grace to heed and to obey the God-given word. To speak even more personally, what is now to be demanded from us is not just our interest or our approval, but nothing less than the recognition of our personal involvement, and the readiness to commit ourselves wholly and for ever to the pursuit of the way which Christ has opened for us.

Reasons for Paying Heed: 2 : 1–4

The word spoken to us by God in Christ is a word to which we simply must pay heed. For it comes to us with compelling authority. First, it was spoken by the Lord Himself, that is, by One who is Himself God. Second, it has been communicated to us by the first-hand testimony of actual eye-witnesses. Third, it was confirmed as divine in origin by accompanying signs and special supernatural activities of the Holy Spirit. There is no doubting or denying that this word is a word from God Himself.

In addition, it is a word for our benefit; a word intended to make ours the enjoyment of God-given salvation. This implies that our condition without it is one of dire peril. This implies also, and

[1] 13 : 22.

inevitably, that to neglect it is not only to fail to enjoy God's best, but also ourselves to have to face the worst. For, as things are, we are in danger; and our condemnation and consequent judgment can only be the greater if, after being enlightened with the knowledge of gospel truth, and given full opportunity to embrace its benefits, we knowingly take no proper interest in what it offers to us. Such deliberate disregard of revealed truth is as much a sinful defiance of its author as deliberate transgression of a divine injunction. The Mosaic economy shows plainly that such defiance is bound to encounter just retribution.

Finally, the matter is the more urgent because the opportunity to embrace salvation will not last for ever. If we do not embrace such benefit while we so easily can, we may find later that we have drifted past it, and are no longer within reach of its enjoyment. Dr. William Barclay points out that the Greek word here translated "to pay attention" can mean "to moor a ship". So "this first verse could be very vividly translated: 'Therefore, we must the more eagerly anchor our lives to the things that we have been taught, lest the ship of life drift past the harbour and be wrecked.' " Dr. Barclay then pertinently adds: "For most of us the threat of life is not so much that we should plunge into disaster, but that we should drift into sin. There are few people who deliberately and in a moment turn their backs on God; there are many who day by day drift farther and farther away from Him."[2]

The Promised Blessings and Their Enjoyment: 3:6b–14; 4:1–4

Here, if we are to be stirred to a full awareness, and to a proper sense of responsibility – and of danger – we need to pause to appreciate the character of the benefits which by the gospel are freely offered to us. God's purpose in Christ is to dwell among us as *his house*[3] or family; or to dwell in us as *his house* or sanctuary. We are chosen and intended to *share in Christ*.[4] The promise still remains open of entering into God's rest.[5] This rest, into which God Himself entered after the creation of the universe, is not just empty inactivity, but rather the satisfaction and repose which rightly follow successful achievement. God's word also witnesses that He

[2] *The Letter to the Hebrews*, p. 13.
[3] 3:6.   [4] 3:14.
[5] See 4:1, and NEB.

intends His people to share His own *sabbath rest*;[6] and, as the writer of this epistle especially emphasizes, God's declared purpose cannot remain for ever unfulfilled.[7]

Scripture records that those to whom the opportunity to enter in was first offered failed to embrace it. It also implies that Canaan, the inheritance into which Joshua led the Israelites, cannot be the promised rest. For, long after his day, God still speaks in Psalm 95 of a present opportunity to enter in.[8] Indeed, God's Spirit is still *today*[9] warning men not to harden their hearts, lest they miss the present opportunity to embrace the divine promise. In addition, we are told that such entrance into rest will have, in principle, the same characteristic in men's experience as in God's. *For whoever enters God's rest also ceases from his labours as God did from his.*[10] Yet, there is here also a radical difference. For God has procured His rest in consequence of His works.[11] But we sinful men are allowed to enjoy it, by God's gift; not by our own achievement, but as the reward of God's work for us.

The Scriptures also indicate very explicitly that the one condition of the enjoyment of such blessing is faith – and faith openly confessed and actively exercised to the end of our earthly pilgrimage. We can enter into our calling as members of Christ's house only if we maintain to the end the outspoken confidence and exulting testimony of our God-given faith as His children.[12] *For we share in Christ, if only we hold our first confidence firm to the end.*[13] *It is we, who have become believers, who enter the rest referred to.*[14]

A Solemn God-given Warning: 3:7–11, 15–19; 4:1, 2, 11

It is just at this point of necessary persistence in faith that failure is possible. It was just at this point that the writer of this epistle was persuaded that his readers were failing; and so urgently needed both warning and encouragement. He realized, too, that the record of what happened to the Israelites in the wilderness provides a solemn God-given warning of the gravity of the peril which may still beset those who have begun to share in the experience of God's salvation.

For these Israelites, *who left Egypt under the leadership of*

[6] 4:9.   [7] See 4:6, 7.   [8] See 4:8.
[9] 4:7.   [10] 4:10.   [11] See 4:4.
[12] See 3:6.   [13] 3:14.   [14] 4:3, NEB.

Moses,[15] had all participated in the decisive beginnings of God-wrought redemption. Their families, under the shed blood of the passover lamb, had found shelter from judgment for their firstborn sons. They had all experienced the benefit of the significant demonstration of God's power at the Red Sea, by which they were delivered and the Egyptians overthrown. Yet, in the wilderness, on the divinely-appointed road to the promised land, with God Himself active to guide and to provide, they hardened their hearts in rebellion, they repeatedly complained, they had to be dealt with by God in disciplinary judgment. The majority[16] of them so displeased God that He could take them no further along the road to the fulfilment of His promises. So of them He swore in His wrath, *They shall never enter my rest.*[17]

Nor was such failure a sudden passing relapse quickly repented of, and from which they soon recovered. It was rather the expression of an attitude which became chronic and deep-seated. Surprising as it is that people who had enjoyed such mercies at God's hand should so react, they became persistently rebellious and disobedient. Although God followed them for forty years with His gracious providences, they showed no responsive understanding of His ways. Their hearts were still as hard, if not harder, *in the rebellion* as *on the day of testing in the wilderness.*[18]

In the original Hebrew of the psalm which is here quoted, these phrases include the place names Meribah and Massah,[19] names which mean "rebellion" or "contention" and "testing" or "proof". In both places, instead of looking in faith to God to provide, the Israelites murmured against Moses, and, by implication, against God Himself, for lack of water. The very fact that the two incidents were one at the end and the other at the beginning of the wilderness wanderings shows how chronic and unchangeable their attitude of resentful unbelief had become.

What we need to appreciate is that the record of their failure stands written in the Scriptures as a permanent God-given warning. Of this Paul said, *Now these things happened to them as a warning, but they were written down for our instruction.*[20] Here the writer of this epistle quotes Psalm 95, which shows how the Israelites' failure has explicitly been given divine sanction as a warning to

[15] 3:16.   [16] See I Cor. 10:1-5.
[17] 3:11.   [18] 3:8.
[19] See Ps. 95:8; Num. 20:13; Exod. 17:7.
[20] I Cor. 10:11.

God's people, and claims for its words a continuing present-day application, as words which the Holy Spirit is still saying today.[21] To quote the rendering by J. B. Phillips, "These words are still being said for our ears to hear."[22]

The Corresponding Peril That Besets Us: 3:12–15; 4:1

The warning afforded by the failure of the Israelites in the wilderness was particularly pertinent to the condition of the first readers of this epistle. For they had lived through the days of an intervention of God in history to deliver His people – an intervention greater than the exodus from Egypt under Moses. They belonged to the generation which had seen the true Lamb of God slain to provide *redemption through his blood, the forgiveness of our trespasses.*[23] They had joined the company of those who had witnessed Christ's resurrection from the dead, and experienced the pentecostal outpouring of the Spirit, with all the accompanying evidences of the working of God's power.[24] If, as seems very probable, this epistle was written shortly before AD 70, and its first readers had been converted to faith in Christ in very early days, at or shortly after Pentecost, then they had been confessed believers in Jesus as the Christ for about forty years. So the one who was writing to them sought to make them directly aware that in the here and now of their present experience the Holy Spirit is in Psalm 95 warning them personally of the perils of their own unbelief.

Nor, as those who believe that Scriptures thus written long ago were inspired by God's Spirit for the permanent instruction of God's people, can we escape facing the truth that this word of warning is also meant for us. There is similar cause for us to *take care* and to *fear.*[25] For in Christ, and by the gospel and its preaching, the same promises of entrance into God-given reward have been extended to us. We have heard the message preached to us. We are here found studying this particular epistle. So we may quote this writer's words as if they were directly written to us, and say, *For good news came to us just as to them.* Nor can we stop there. For he goes on, *But the message which they heard did not benefit them, because it did not meet with faith in the hearers.*[26]

[21] See 3:7 f.   [22] 3:15.
[23] Eph. 1:7.   [24] See 2:4.
[25] See 3:12; 4:1.   [26] 4:2.

This, then, is a warning that we, too, are clearly meant to take to heart; namely that it is possible to be intimately acquainted with the promises of God, it is possible to be generally aware that they are intended for our enjoyment, and yet to be left out of the experience of their fulfilment – or to *be judged to have failed to reach it*.[27]

To suggest an illustration of the writer's possible meaning here, we are like intending passengers standing on a station platform alongside the railway train which has been provided to take us to the desired destination. Perhaps we have got out of the train at some stopping place on the journey. We know that we are intended, and by God's grace freely invited, to continue to travel by the train to the journey's end. The urgent demand of the present moment is to get in. The peril, if we fail to do so while the opportunity lasts, is that the train will move on without us, and we shall find ourselves "left behind". *Therefore, while the promise of entering his rest remains, let us fear lest* – yes, lest we fail either fully to obtain what God has promised or to finish the course which God desires us to pursue.

For, in the last analysis, there are only two possibilities. If we are not inside, enjoying God's rest, we shall be outside; and, by God's solemn irrevocable oath, shut out for ever. For it is God Himself who has said of such, *They shall never enter my rest*.[28] So, if we do not by our active and sustained response to God's word become evidences of the blessing to be enjoyed by all who fully trust and obey, we shall fall by the roadside, and become examples of the judgment that overtakes the disobedient, like the Israelites, *whose bodies fell in the wilderness*.[29] *Therefore, while the promise of entering his rest remains, let us fear lest* – yes, lest *we fall away from the living God*.[30]

Lessons to be Learnt: 3 : 10, 12, 13, 19

Such examples of failure as are recorded in the Scriptures for our admonition will only serve their purpose if we are prepared to use our minds, to appreciate how and why these people were *unable to enter*[31] God's rest. For failure properly to use their minds was a fundamental cause of their wrong attitude towards God. They

---

[27] 4 : 1.
[29] 3 : 17. Cf. 4 : 11b and RV mg.
[31] 3 : 19.

[28] 3 : 11; 4 : 5.
[30] 4 : 1; 3 : 12.

became wholly mistaken in their thinking. They completely failed to grasp the purpose of God's dealings with them, or why He chose to lead them in the way He did, through the many trials of a wilderness experience. Consequently God was indignant with them and said of them, *Their hearts are forever astray; they would not discern my ways.*[32]

As professing Christians we need to learn that life's journey is all the time under God's providence being made to serve His purpose of trying us out in order to discover the real attitude and practical reaction of our minds to His word and His way, and thus to Himself.[33] For the privilege of coming within the sphere of God's special activity in grace and salvation, in revelation and redemption, in providence and discipline, as the Israelites did, means that we can no longer continue as we were; either we go on in faith to become better, or we draw back in rebellion to become worse.

For our safety we need to become fully aware of the perils that beset up; the peril, to begin with, of growing stubborn,[34] of hardening our hearts against God – against His word and His way; and the peril, in the end, of nothing less than complete apostasy, of falling away from the living God,[35] of choosing to go our own way, and of saying, in effect, "I have finished with God."

Similarly we need to appreciate the underlying causes of such a wrong reaction. They are of two kinds; from outside, from the things which we see and hear in the world around us, there is the apparent attractiveness of the path of disobedience, or *the deceitfulness of sin;*[36] and from inside, as the source from which wrong reaction takes its rise, there is *an evil, unbelieving heart,*[37] consequent upon the failure to hold fast to our confidence in God. As the writer of this epistle thus emphasizes, it is the truth about this last evil that is the outstanding lesson to be learnt from the failure of the Israelites in the wilderness. The chief cause of the tragedy was unbelief. *So we see that they were unable to enter because of unbelief.*[38]

Appropriate Precautionary Measures: 3:12, 13; 4:1, 11

The issues at stake here are so great, and the perils that beset us are

[32] 3:10, NEB.   [33] See Deut. 8:2.
[34] 3:8, NEB.   [35] 3:12.
[36] 3:13.   [37] 3:12.
[38] 3:19.

C

so grave, that only the foolish or those already fatally hardened will remain unmoved. We ought surely to be asking ourselves what we should do to avoid spiritual disaster. The simplest and best precaution against slipping back is actively to devote all one's interest and effort to going on; and, in consequence, to be ever on the alert to hear God's voice and to express faith in Him by prompt and persistent obedience. So the writer concludes his present appeal with an obviously paradoxical but very relevant exhortation. *Let us then make every effort to enter that rest.*[39]

In addition, this writer indicates that this is a sphere of practical danger in which as fellow-pilgrims Christians ought to help one another; and the more so as we are called to make this journey together in the company of God's people. So he exhorts the many – *the brethren* – to take care lest unbelief appears in the heart of any single one of their number.[40] He enjoins them to *exhort one another every day* in order that no single one of them may be hardened by sin's deceitfulness.[41] Here surely is a very practical indication of an intended profit to be found in Christian fellowship. We are meant to care for one another, to encourage one another, to join with our fellow-Christians in helping the brother who might otherwise be overwhelmed by temptation and sin.[42] It should be the concern of all who are making the journey to see that not a single one of our number should be found in the final reckoning to have been left behind. We are to fear, not just each for himself, but for one another.[43]

Nor is that all. For the Scripture record indicates that full entrance by the Israelites into the promised land was not achieved by individuals like Joshua and Caleb, one by one, as each became spiritually ready to take possession. It was a fulfilment possible only for the community. They entered in together, when all were ready. The unbelieving and the disobedient held up the enjoyment of fulfilment by all the rest. They had first to be dealt with by God in disciplinary judgment and removed. So, if we desire to share in the possession by the Church of God of the blessings which He has promised to His people not one by one but as a corporate fellowship, this exhortation is of direct practical relevance. For it tells us all to be on the alert lest any one of our number hinder the progress or start a move in the wrong direction.[44]

[39] 4:11, NEB.   [40] 3:12.   [41] 3:13.
[42] Cf. Gal. 6:1, 2.   [43] See 4:1.   [44] Cf. 12:15.

Our Inescapable Responsibility: 4:12, 13

All words have behind them as their source the person who is their author. Also, when words are rightly used they reveal and commit their author; they promise or imply complementary action; they are completed by deeds. "To the Jews . . . a word was a power, a force which went forth and did things."[45] If we say of someone, "You cannot trust his words," we mean, "You cannot trust him." The word is an expression of the character of the man himself. This is equally true of God's words. Because God lives and abides, because He does not die or disappear, so His word is *living and abiding*.[46] It never becomes obsolete, out-of-date, or a dead-letter. He is still active to fulfil it.[47] So, says the writer of this epistle, *the word of God is living and active*.

Consequently, although God's promise concerning entrance into His rest was first spoken long ago, it is still a vital and operative word, offering to us present benefit by its fulfilment. It is not just the word which long ago the psalmist wrote for the people of his day, but rather it is the present urgent word to us of God the Spirit. Therefore, to reject this word is to *refuse him who is speaking*;[48] and to make rebellion against this word our settled attitude is to *fall away from the living God*.[49]

Also, by the word which He speaks to us God provokes to active expression the real desires and intentions of our hearts. In this way He finds out by His dealings with us and by His demands upon us whether we will walk in His ways or not; whether at heart we are obedient or unbelieving.

These two verses, which we are here considering,[50] begin by referring to *the word* which comes to us from God. They end in the Greek by mentioning *the word* which must be given back to God by us. For, since God has spoken to us, we are inescapably involved in dealings with Him. We are made answerable, and must give back our account. Nor can we avoid such an encounter. For no one is or can be hidden from God. Whether we will or not, we must in the end appear before Him virtually naked, and completely exposed to His gaze. The account we give then will be determined by the response we make now.

45 W. Barclay, *op. cit.*, p. 34; cf. Isa. 55:10, 11.
46 I Pet. 1:23.   47 See Num. 23:19.
48 12:25.   49 3:12.   50 4:12, 13.

Finally, what in this epistle is particularly emphasized is that the person who thus confronts us with God's living and active word, and to whom, in the end, as the Judge of the secrets of all hearts, we must give our answer, is none other than Jesus, the Son of God. So, lest we hear from His lips then God's word of excluding judgment – *They shall never enter my rest:*[51] *I never knew you; depart from me, you evil-doers*[52] – what is of the most urgent importance is that now – *while it is said, "Today"*[53] – in the day of continuing opportunity to believe and obey, we should *hear his voice,*[53] and find in Him for our full salvation the living and abiding fulfilment of all that His word promises

[51] 3:11; 4:5.
[52] Matt. 7:23.
[53] 3:15.

Five

Our Great High Priest

4:14–5:10; 7:1–8:6

THE WRITER OF THIS EPISTLE HAS ALREADY MADE HIS READERS aware that he desires them particularly to *consider Jesus* as their *high priest*.[1] He has explicitly indicated that this was a main purpose of the incarnation of the Son of God —to enable Him to function as our high priest. *Therefore he had to be made like his brethren in every respect, so that he might become a merciful and faithful high priest.*[2]

Now, in what is almost a fresh beginning in the middle of his writing, he sets himself to make detailed exposition of this truth his chief concern. Indeed, later he goes so far as to confess that this truth concerning the character of the high priest whom *we have*,[3] and can therefore call ours, is *the chief point*[4] which he is striving to drive home. Here[5] he begins by asserting that our possession, as Christians, of such *a great high priest* as *Jesus, the Son of God*, Himself already enthroned in heaven, is itself a decisive reason for continuing in the faith, and holding fast to our confession of Him as the Christ of God.

Encouragement to Take Active Personal Interest: 4:14–16

Before engaging in more exposition of doctrinal truth, the writer briefly exhorts his readers not only to appreciate the benefits which these truths make available for our enjoyment but also personally to appropriate them. Christ, he asserts, is doubly worthy of our confidence and our confession, first, because of His unique person, and second, because of the successful accomplishment of His work on our behalf. For He is *great* in His essential nature as God incarnate, as *Jesus, the Son of God*. Also, in His work as our high priest what He has achieved is great. For He has passed through the

[1] 3:1. [2] 2:17.
[3] 4:14; 8:1. [4] 8:1, RV.
[5] 4:14.

created heavens *into heaven itself, now to appear in the presence
of God on our behalf.*[6] *So let us hold fast our confession.*[7]

Nor is that all. For, in addition, God has enthroned Him at His
own right hand, so that He has unlimited power to minister to our
needs; and, because He won entrance on our behalf, as our high
priest, the way stands open for us to approach the throne of God.
Also, if we do come, we shall find in Him both understanding sympathy and bountiful generosity. For, because of His own earthly
experience as Man, He understands our limitations and our frailty
as finite creatures. He knows every form of temptation that can
beset us; for He was similarly tempted. His triumph, as One from
first to last *without sin,*[8] has been won in the field of our conflict
and our need. So He is fully qualified to extend to us both merciful
compassion and appropriate practical help.

There are, in consequence, four complementary activities in
which we now can and ought to share. The first is to come, to
draw near, to exercise the privilege of priests, and ourselves to enter
the heavenly sanctuary of the presence of God. The second is to
come *boldly,*[9] to draw near *with confidence,* with daring out-
spokenness, because we are coming to a merciful high priest. The
third is to find in experience that the very throne of God is not a
throne of terror, but that, by the enthronement there at God's right
hand of One who is our high priest, it has been transformed for us
into *the throne of grace.* The fourth is to *receive,* as gifts from our
Saviour's own hands, mercy for our sinfulness and our weaknesses,
and help suited to the need of the hour, whatever it may be. This is
how true Christian life begins, and how daily it should be sustained,
by coming to the throne of grace to our high priest, Jesus the Son of
God. *Let us then . . . draw near.*

Clearly, the more we learn about the person and work and ability
to save to the uttermost of our great high priest, the richer our
experience of His mercy and His enabling grace ought to be. This is
why the writer of this epistle is so eager that we should study
what he writes, not just for the information of our minds, but also
and more particularly for the enrichment and transformation of our
lives.

[6] 9:24.
[7] 4:14.
[8] 4:15, AV.
[9] 4:16, AV.

Qualifications and Activities Essential in a High Priest: 5:1-4

The distinctive work for whose performance a high priest is appointed is *to act on behalf of men in relation to God.* Obviously no one can do this properly unless he himself is a man, one *chosen from among men.* He needs to have as a true man a capacity for full fellow-feeling with those whom he is to represent, and whose cause he is to undertake. He must be ready and able to *deal gently with the ignorant and wayward* or "erring", to adopt (as the Greek word suggests) an attitude towards men, when they get involved in folly and defiled by sin, that is neither too lenient nor too severe. For it is the sinfulness of men with which it is his task to deal. As high priest it is his work to offer sacrifice for sin. And as a man like other men, himself *beset with weakness* and involved in sinning, *he is bound to offer sacrifice for his own sins as well as for those of the people.*

Nor dare he presume to take upon himself the task of thus appearing before God to make propitiation for the sins of men. He must, in the first place, be *called by God, just as Aaron was.* It must be clear that God is willing for such a ministry to be undertaken, and that He is pleased that this particular man should undertake it.

Christ's Corresponding Qualifications and Activities:
5:5-10; 7:27; 8:1-6.

Judged by these recognized standards Christ is now shown to be properly qualified and fully active as our high priest. First, the genuineness of His humanity and the extent of His capacity for sympathy have already been indicated.[10] But additional evidence is here provided concerning the character and the significance of His earthly human experience during *the days of His flesh.*[11] The truth is stressed that, although He was God the Son, as Man He learnt the full meaning in outworked practice of obedient submission to God's direction. He learnt this from the demands and the discipline of a genuine human experience. This involved Him at times, particularly, for instance, in the garden of Gethsemane, in an agony of spiritual conflict, in which *with loud cries and tears,* and in a spirit

[10] See 2:9, 14, 16-18; 4:15.
[11] 5:7-9.

both of triumphant faith in God's power, and of reverent submission to God's choice, He sought that God's will should be done.
It was by means of such experience that He became fully mature in
human character, and acquired complete competence to function
as the Saviour of other men; from whom He now demands the same
kind of responsive obedience as He Himself gave to God. So here,
for our encouragement, let us learn that, no matter what we may
have to face of earthly trial or pain, Jesus, from His deeper and
triumphant experience of similar suffering, is able fully to sym-
pathize and unfailingly to save. The *salvation* which He can thus
make ours is, too, more than mere passing relief granted to a few
privileged souls. It is *eternal*; and for *all who obey him*.

In the second place, Christ can be of help to us as high priest only
if He offers sacrifice for sins. The necessity of His fulfilment of
such ministry is fully recognized by this writer.[12] But he does not
deal with this ministry of Christ until later in his epistle, because
the subject needs expanded treatment in order to indicate the
significant ways in which Christ's ministry of this kind was not only
similar to, but also different from, the familiar ministry of Jewish
priests and their offering of animal sacrifices.

Before he expounds these truths in detail[13] he introduces a number of brief statements in order to begin to make his readers aware
of the differences to be appreciated. It will be enough for us to
notice these now, and, with the writer of the epistle, to leave more
detailed consideration till later. These statements indicate that
Christ had no need to offer for His own sin, because He was sinless;
that the sacrifice He offered was not an animal but Himself; that
He has no need to make repeated offerings, because He did all that
was necessary once for all by His one offering; and that His offering
was not made like the Jewish sacrifices in the earthly sanctuary of
the Jewish temple, in which, as not being a Levite, Jesus would
have had no right to function as a priest at all, but that it was
offered in relation to the true tabernacle, in order to win access for
men into the heavenly sanctuary of God's presence.[14]

In the third place, *Christ did not exalt himself to be made a high
priest*.[15] He was appointed by God. In proof of this the writer here
quotes two statements from the Old Testament,[16] from psalms

[12] See 8 : 3.   [13] In 9 : 1–10 : 18.
[14] See 7 : 27; 8 : 2, 4–6.   [15] 5 : 5.
[16] From Ps. 2 : 7; 110 : 4.

which are unmistakably messianic — statements which in the Scriptures concerned are said to be made by God to Christ. Both psalms prophetically refer to God's enthronement of His Christ in the heavenly Zion and at His own right hand. The interest here is in the fact that He was so enthroned as our high priest.

The first statement indicates that He has His own inherent right to be where He is, both as Himself from eternity God the Son, and also as Himself now the glorified Man, raised from the grave and exalted to the throne by God. The second statement adds that, thus put by God upon the throne, He is to function there for men as their *priest*; and that, because as God He cannot die, and because as the glorified Man death has no more dominion over Him, His function as men's priest will be *for ever*, or without end. It is, too, because of these characteristics, which made Him so different from the Levitical priests, that He is *designated by God a high priest after the order of Melchizedek*.[17]

A High Priest after the Order of Melchizedek: 5:6, 10, 11; 6:19, 20; 7:1–3, 15–17, 20, 21

This is a subject concerning which the writer of this epistle indicates that he has *much to say*. He also finds it *hard to explain* to his readers, because of their backward and unsatisfactory spiritual condition.[18] So, before proceeding with detailed exposition, he turns aside to give his readers fresh practical exhortation.[19] It may, of course, be similarly desirable today that, before they proceed with the study of this theme about Melchizedek, some readers should face, because they need it, a searching challenge concerning their own spiritual condition. So, any who, for their own good rightly prefer to follow the exact sequence of the epistle itself, should at this point read the next chapter (in which 5:11–6:20 is expounded) before they go on to read the remainder of this present chapter which deals with our Lord's high priesthood.

The introduction of Melchizedek to provide a pattern, illustrating, as a priest, the character and position (or *order*) of Christ's own priesthood, is very remarkable. Not only is the illustration taken from the Old Testament,[20] but also the Old Testament itself authorizes its use, and prophetically declares that God's Christ is to

[17] 5:10.
[18] 5:11.
[19] See 5:11–6:20.
[20] See Gen., 14:17–20.

be a priest for ever after this order.[21] The writer of this epistle puts it this way. He says that *this Melchizedek* has been *made like unto the Son of God*:[22] not, let us notice like unto Jesus; nor that the Son of God has been made like unto Melchizedek.

This implies that, whatever may have been actually true of the historical person Melchizedek, in the scriptural record he is so presented as to reflect some of the characteristics – particularly the unique divine characteristics – of the coming Messiah, with special reference to His function as a priest. This is achieved as much by what the Scriptures do not record about Melchizedek, as by what they say. Commenting on this Dr. W. H. Griffith Thomas appropriately declared, "The fact that Melchizedek is thus conformed to our Lord is an instance of the remarkable foresight associated with Scripture, and is a proof of its possession of a depth of meaning which could only come as the result of divine inspiration."[23]

Let us notice the development of three ideas, already seen to be implied by the form of God's appointment of Christ as high priest. First, Melchizedek's right to be a priest at all is not based, like that of Jewish priests, on his descent or genealogy. He appears as a priest in his own right *without* (mention of) *father or mother or genealogy*. This is similarly true of Christ, because He is God the Son and Himself the sinless Man and the Lord's anointed servant, directly and personally chosen of God. His right to function is inherent in His person, and not derived from other men.

In the second place, Melchizedek *has neither beginning of days nor end of life*. Neither his birth nor his death is recorded. As a figure on the page of the scriptural record he both appears once in history, and also abides continually or *continues a priest for ever*. In this, too, he is made like the Son of God, who has appeared once in history, but is as God from eternity to eternity. He lives for ever and cannot die. So His ability to function as our high priest is endless or interminable. A day will never dawn when He will cease to be alive, available and active.

In the third place, Melchizedek is also king; first, as his name indicates, *king of righteousness*, and also, as Salem the name of his city declares, *king of peace*. This, too, corresponds to the position and character of our great high priest. For He is a king upon His

[21] See Ps., 110:4. [22] 7:3, RV and AV.
[23] *"Let us go on"*, p. 87.

throne, in a way in which no Levitical priest ever was or could be; and on the ground of His work done in righteousness, He is able to bless men with His peace.

This last characteristic is true of Christ only because of His earthly work as Man. His true humanity is essential to His priesthood. While, as Son of God He lives for ever, it is only through becoming *Jesus*, the Man, and as *a forerunner* entering into *the inner shrine on our behalf* that He became in realized function our high priest. But once He had thus entered and was enthroned, Jesus, the Man, became *a high priest for ever after the order of Melchizedek*,[24] able henceforth and without end to administer the benefits of His finished work of atoning sacrifice to all who draw near. Like Melchizedek meeting Abraham, He meets with us and brings forth for our sustenance and refreshment His gifts of *bread and wine*.[25]

As the Scriptures quoted in this epistle explicitly emphasize,[26] it is also of very pertinent significance that it is only as *Jesus, the Son of God*,[27] – only as the God-Man, in His humanity already crucified, risen and exalted to God's right hand – that Christ is hailed by God as now a priest for ever and a priest of the Melchizedek order. For, as the writer of this epistle points out later, the Levitical priests were ever striving to fulfil priestly ministry but were never able properly to complete it and achieve its goal.[28] They were like a woman repeatedly trying to bring to the birth, but never able to bring forth. Such a woman, though clearly occupied in the activity necessary to motherhood, would never reach the point where she could be hailed as "A mother at last"; and indeed, by such an achievement, "A mother for ever", never again capable of being described as childless.

Similarly, in contrast to the Levitical priests, whose animal sacrifices could never take away sin,[29] Jesus in His death achieved what was necessary to put away sin.[30] He then won access for men to God's presence. His primary task as a would-be priest was accomplished. So it was that at this point of His realized triumph, when as Man He was by God raised from the dead and exalted to the throne, He was hailed and acclaimed by God – indeed, solemnly instituted by an oath[31] – as now a priest indeed, a priest for ever,

[24] See 6:19, 20. [25] See Gen. 14:17, 18. [26] Ps. 2:7 and 110:4.
[27] 4:14. [28] 10:11. [29] 10:1-4.
[30] 9:26. [31] 7:20, 21.

and a priest able from His throne to give blessings and gifts to men;
and so a *priest for ever after the order of Melchizedek.*[32]

Scriptural Indication that Such a New Priest Should Arise: 7:4–22

Since the Jews had a priesthood, and a priesthood divinely instituted
and authorized, they appeared to possess strong ground for believing that any other priesthood was unnecessary, and that any better
priesthood was impossible. There was need, therefore, carefully to
explain the ways in which another and a better priest was required;
and that his provision was itself a fulfilment of God's recognizable
intention.

First, the writer of the epistle makes further use of the illustration
provided by Melchizedek in order to show that a better priest is
possible. For Melchizedek was clearly greater than Abraham, and,
by implication, greater than his descendant Levi, the ancestor of all
Jewish priests. For Melchizedek both received tithes from Abraham,
and gave blessing to Abraham; and both activities suggest that he is
greater than Abraham, and consequently, as a priest, greater than
Levi. Also, since God has prophetically declared that His Christ is to
be a priest of the Melchizedek order or status, He must as priest be
greater than Aaron and the Levitical priests.

In the second place, if God has spoken in prophecy, as He has, of
establishing a new order of priesthood, this unmistakably implies
that the existing Levitical priesthood is inadequate to achieve the
true goal of priestly activity. For, *if perfection had been attainable
through the Levitical priesthood,*[33] no such new step would have
been necessary. Also, because the institution of priesthood is itself
part of a divinely-ordered constitution governing God's relations
with His people, any such complete change in the priesthood must
inevitably be accompanied by a change in the whole constitution.[34]
The covenant which God formerly made with His people must
therefore be superseded by a better one – better because it will
succeed where the existing covenant had failed, better because,
through the new priesthood, it will enable the people of God to
attain "perfection" and thus to share fully in the realization of
God's purpose for them.

This is exactly what has happened in the coming of Christ. He

[32] 7:17.   [33] 7:11.
[34] See 7:12.

clearly has no connexion with the Levitical priesthood, and no right to function as a priest in the Jewish temple or tabernacle. For He *belonged to another tribe, from which no one has ever served at the altar. For it is evident that our Lord was descended from Judah, and in connexion with that tribe Moses said nothing about priests*.[35] Also, He was established as a priest on different grounds; not by reason of His physical descent, nor by necessary consecration through the proper fulfilment of ritual requirements, but simply because in Himself He possessed *the power of an indestructible life*.[36] Death could not triumph over Him.

The need for Christ's appearing as a better high priest and the need for the putting on one side of the old covenant were thus undeniable. For the existing system has proved itself in practice weak and useless, unable to reach the intended goal – the goal of giving sinful men full access to God's presence, and realized "perfection" or true fulfilment in His service.[37] In Christ this *better hope is introduced*. As high priest of the new order Jesus is *the surety of a better covenant*.[38] His right thus to function for our benefit, and henceforth to function without fail for ever, is guaranteed not only by God's word appointing Him to this office, but also by the added and unalterable confirmation of a divine oath, declaring by the highest and most solemn of sanctions that Christ is divinely authorized to function as a *priest for ever*.[39]

His is the Power of an Indestructible Life: 7 : 15, 16, 23–25, 27

Christ's power as priest to meet our every need and to accomplish our salvation to its full completion is particularly to be found in His *endless life*.[40] This means, in contrast to the former Levitical priests, who *were prevented by death from continuing in office*, that Christ *holds his priesthood permanently*.[41] No second priest will ever be needed to take His place and to continue the functions which He now discharges. Nor can any one ever take this office from Him. His priesthood is non-transferable or *unchangeable*.[42] *Consequently he is able for all time to save those who draw near to God through him*.[43] While, under the old system, men were appointed as high priests who were limited in their capacity by

[35] 7:13, 14. [36] 7:16. [37] 7:18, 19.
[38] 7:22. [39] 7:20, 21. [40] 7:16, AV and RV.
[41] 7:23, 24. [42] 7:24, AV and RV. [43] 7:25.

their human weakness, the One who is now appointed to this office, and confirmed in it by an oath of God, will never fail through such frailty. For He is God the Son; and, as Man and priest, He is made absolutely and unchangeably perfect and competent for evermore.

Here it is important also to appreciate the exact character of His present priestly ministry. He is no longer offering sacrifice for sins. For this He has no need to do. *He did this once for all when he offered up himself.*[44] What He now does is to fulfil complementary priestly ministries which are made possible by His successful performance of the primary task of all priestly activity, which is to make propitiation for sin and to give men access to God. The illustration of motherhood may again help our understanding. The indispensable initial achievement which permanently constitutes a woman as a mother is to give birth to a child. That is how she truly becomes a mother. But the function of motherhood does not end with this successful achievement. It is a mother's complementary task to care for the needs and the nurture, for the safety and the well-being (that is, in scriptural language, for the full salvation) of the child to whom she has given birth. Similarly Christ is permanently constituted as men's high priest by His successful performance of the necessary sacrifice for sins. The way of access to God now permanently stands open, and does not have again to be opened up. But, when sinners avail themselves of the benefits of Christ's work, and *draw near to God through Him,* there is still a priestly ministry which He waits to fulfil. It is *to make intercession for them;*[45] that is, to speak to God on their behalf, to plead their cause, to gainsay any who would condemn them as sinners and thus oppose their right to appear in God's presence. His intercession for us thus ensures that our prayers will be answered.[46] Indeed, He is authorized by God from the throne in grace to extend mercy and grace, and to give blessing and gifts, to all who draw near to God through Him.[47]

It is to fulfil this ministry that Christ *always lives,* or now as our high priest *continues for ever.*[48] "To all eternity He remains the introducer of men to God." So writes Dr. William Barclay. And as he goes on to point out, "the verb here used for 'to continue' means *to remain in the capacity of a servant.*" For instance, "Gregory of Nazianzen provides in his will that his daughters will *remain* with their mother so long as she is alive. They are to stay with her and

[44] 7:27.   [45] 7:25.   [46] Cf., Rom., 8:33, 34.
[47] See 4:16.   [48] 7:24, 25.

be her help and her support. . . . So when the writer to the Hebrews says that Jesus *remains for ever*, there is wrapped up in that phrase the amazing thought that *Jesus is for ever at the service of men.* . . . That is why He is the complete Saviour."[49]

So We Have a High Priest Exactly Suited to Our Need: 7 : 26–28; 8 : 1

It is these truths about Jesus, the Son of God, as our great high priest that reveal God's all-sufficient provision for our full salvation. *It was fitting*, declares the writer of this epistle, *that we should have such a high priest*; and, which is very much more, *The point in what we are saying is this: we have such a high priest.*

The qualities which make Him competent to function effectively are that He is Himself sinless – *holy, blameless unstained, separated from sinners*; that He has already accomplished once for all the necessary initial work of making propitiation for sin; and that He possesses the three characteristics already emphasized in the comparison with Melchizedek; namely, personal deity as God the Son, human glorification as the exalted Man, *made perfect for ever*, and enthronement in the place of supremacy and power, *at the right hand of the throne of the Majesty in heaven*.

Finally, the amazing truth is that this high priest is ours; that He is available to be acknowledged, approached, confided in, and used; that He waits, always living to fulfil His gracious saving and sanctifying ministries for all who come to God through Him, and for each one of us every fresh time we come. As Christians we need no longer fear as inevitable the awful tragedy (illustrated by the Israelites in the wilderness) of failing to continue to the end, of coming sadly to grief in the middle. For *we have a great priest over the house of God*.[50] He is not only *the pioneer* but also the *perfecter*[51] of faith's activity, able, as we look to Him, not only to bring us into God's presence for the first time, and to make our peace with God and new life in the Spirit, but able also to bring us safely to the end of the course in the *race that is set before us*.[51]

[49] *The Letter to the Hebrews*, p. 88 : Dr. Barclay's italics.
[50] 10 : 21.
[51] 12 : 1, 2.

Six

The Challenge to Go on to Maturity

5:11–6:20

IN THIS SECTION OF THE EPISTLE THE WRITER DIRECTLY TACKLES the spiritual condition and practical needs of its intended readers. He confronts them with blunt and urgent exhortation. We shall therefore study such a section to the greatest profit only if we are willing to submit ourselves to some corresponding self-examination, and to apply to ourselves the writer's words of rebuke, encouragement and exhortation.

This is the third hortatory passage in this epistle. The first (in 2:1–4) combined a positive exhortation with an urgent practical warning. *We must pay the closer attention to what we have heard. How shall we escape if we neglect such a great salvation?*

The second hortatory passage (in 3:7–4:13) developed these two emphases at greater length with the history of the Israelites in the wilderness as a divinely-provided illustration. *Therefore, while the promise of entering his rest remains, let us fear lest any of you be judged to have failed to reach it.*[1] *Let us therefore strive to enter that rest, that no one fall by the same sort of disobedience.*[2]

In this third hortatory passage (in 5:11–6:20) the same combination of exhortation and warning occurs; and it is made, if possible, even more personal and urgent by a pointed opening rebuke. *You have become dull of hearing.*[3] *Let us . . . go on to maturity.*[4] *For it is impossible to restore again to repentance those who have once been enlightened . . . if they then commit apostasy.*[5] Here is truth for us to apply to ourselves concerning the pathway divinely ordained for the redeemed community. God intends that we should make it a road of progress. But this demands sustained faith and obedience. Also, for any who repeatedly refuse such response, and increasingly harden their hearts in unbelief, the same pathway of spiritual privilege can become a place of peril and even of actual apostasy, to their great damage and eternal loss.

[1] 4:1. [2] 4:11. [3] 5:11.
[4] 6:1. [5] 6:4–6.

Evidences of Failure 5:11-14

The writer felt such deep concern because his readers were plainly spiritually degenerate. They had lost their first love and enthusiasm for the things of Christ. They had *become dull of hearing*, or insensitive to the practical demands of divinely-revealed truth. They were slow-moving in their obedience to the God-given word. For "hearing" here means not just "listening" with passing interest but "answering" in active response.

Consequently their spiritual development had been arrested. They had failed to grow up. They were victims of a kind of infantile paralysis. So, although they were Christians of long-standing, who ought by this time to be teaching others, they seemed to be like infants once again in need of simple elementary instruction, and quite incapable of digesting the solid food of more advanced teaching. For their spiritual faculties were enfeebled, or remained undeveloped, through lack of proper use and exercise.

We may do well at this point to examine ourselves by the same test. For the quality as well as the quantity of spiritual food which we regularly take itself provides an indication of the measure of our spiritual growth and vitality. For Christian maturity is acquired not just through the passing of the years since we accepted Christ, but through practical experience and training. Progress depends upon the exercise of our spiritual senses in moral discernment. Three stages of growth are here distinguished. Spiritual babes or children can take only milk and have to be fed. Spiritual adults can digest solid food and have learnt to feed themselves. As those instructed by *the word of righteousness* they are skilled in making moral distinctions. They show in their conduct that they have acquired the ability to "refuse the evil and choose the good".[6] Teachers, which by this time these readers ought to have become, go one stage further. They – as we may say (using the same illustration) – learn by practice how to select, prepare and serve up suitable food for others. The question for us is – in which of these three classes would the writer of this epistle put you and me?

The Way of Progress: 5:14; 6:1-3

God's purpose in Christ for His children is "perfection" or growth

[6] See Isa. 7:16; contrast Deut. 1:39.

D

to maturity. This concerns both thought and practice. Also, while God permits, and the day of saving grace still lasts, spiritual degeneration can and ought to be remedied. So, far from making their degenerate condition a reason for not attempting to give them more advanced teaching, this writer exhorts his readers to join him in making progress. *Let us*, he says, *go on to maturity*.

The very word he uses – literally, "let us be borne along", like a ship by the wind, or like prophets by God's Spirit[7] – indicates that we are not left to our own strength and resources. It suggests that, if we will but set our course in God's way, and spread our sails, the wind of God's Spirit will carry us forward.

On the other hand, with people in such an unsatisfactory spiritual condition, it is inappropriate, so this writer asserts, to set himself to lay the foundation all over again. In other words, the remedy is not, as we might say, to have an evangelistic mission in order to get them all truly converted. For they have already made a beginning of new life in Christ; and such people, once saved, cannot be regenerated a second time; no more than a child, physically damaged by a paralyzing disease, can start life afresh and go back and be born again. Rather the best must now be made of the powers and potentialities which still remain. Similarly with Christians, whose spiritual life has become diseased or degenerate and stunted in growth, the remedy is not a second new birth. Rather the life in Christ which is already theirs must be given more exercise, food and expression, more nurture, care and outlet; unless of course, the inactivity and consequent paralysis or atrophy are so chronic and deep-seated that such remedial treatment is no longer possible. The way to find out how much improvement is still possible is to make the attempt to go forward. So in such circumstances let this, too, be our resolution. *This will we do if God permits*.

The Only Ultimate Alternative: 6:4–8

If people, who have had such God-given privileges, will not "have faith unto the saving of the soul",[8] there is only one ultimate alternative – fatally and irrevocably to "draw back unto perdition".[9] The choice for them lies between going on to maturity or completely dropping out. Nor with any who do drop out is it possible

[7] See Acts 27:15; 2 Pet. 1:21.
[8] 10:39. RV.   [9] 10:39. AV.

to begin again and relay the foundation a second time. For all, who by deliberate apostasy thus get into a condition in which to start afresh might well seem appropriate, cannot enjoy a similar second opportunity to repent and to believe; for they have already sinned against the witness of God's Spirit, they have rejected God-given light, they have sided with those who disowned and crucified the Son of God, they have brought fresh reproach on His name, and by their apostasy have put him to an open shame. Such can expect nothing but God's judgment. Of them John Calvin wrote, "Such men are deprived, as they deserve, of the Spirit of God, and are given over to a reprobate mind."

Many think that there can be no question that the phrases of verses 4 and 5 describe those who are regenerate; and that the language of verse 6 indicates a complete disowning of Christ, a deliberate and decisive abandonment of the Christian faith and confession. "These four statements," wrote Dr. Griffith Thomas concerning verses 4 and 5, "clearly imply a real and definite spiritual experience. It does not seem possible to interpret these phrases of illumination only, of light rather than life." "Every prominent word used is found applied to believers in other parts of the New Testament."[10] Also, when the writer of the epistle adds, "If they shall fall away,"[11] "it is no ordinary or general fall, but a deliberate apostasy, not backsliding but wilful departure."[12]

However, the writer of the epistle equally clearly, so far at least as his readers are concerned, has only a supposed case before him. "For to prevent his supposition from becoming a reality is the earnest aim of the whole epistle, and especially of this passage."[13] In the verses concerned he significantly uses not the second person but the third, and writes not "if you", but "if they", and, in strong contrast, he immediately adds, *though we speak thus, yet in your case, beloved, we feel sure of better things that belong to salvation.*[14]

One may illustrate the truth here indicated by thinking of an adult saying to a child, as they walk together along a path near a cliff edge, "If you slip over the edge you will be killed; it will be impossible to save you." But, at the same time, his presence and watchful care are the guarantee that such a disaster will not occur.

[10] Cf. 3:1; 10:32.   [11] 6:6.
[12] *"Let us go on"*, pp. 72, 73.
[13] A. B. Davidson, Hebrews Commentary, p. 122.
[14] 6:9.

Similarly here, while the spiritual peril is real, and the warning true and rightly emphasized, there is ground for believing, of those whom the Lord has begun to save, that the fatal fall which is so possible for them will never happen. Did not the Lord Himself say of His own sheep, *"They shall never perish"?*[15] Their final salvation is not determined by their own works but guaranteed by God's grace and faithfulness.

But, as far as the use we make as Christians of our earthly lives is concerned, it is the practical test that is decisive, and will be determinative of God's judgment. *You will know them by their fruits.*[16] Those who, by the response of faith and obedience, become, by God's grace, fruitful to His glory will receive God's blessing and reward. Those who, given the same opportunities and privileges, harden their hearts in disobedient self-will, and metaphorically speaking bear nothing but thorns and thistles, will scarcely escape God's curse; their worthless earthly works will be burned in the fire of God's judgment; and they, as Paul puts it, will suffer loss and themselves be saved only as through fire.[17] So there is double cause for paying heed; not only to receive reward but also to avoid suffering loss.

Since the section here expounded is admittedly difficult of interpretation, and expositors do not all agree as to its particular reference and exact meaning, it may be helpful to some to suggest a somewhat different interpretation, an interpretation which does not involve the assumption that those who commit apostasy are already regenerate.

We may find ground for this interpretation in what our Lord said about the cities in which His mighty works were done,[18] and about the people who enjoyed the divine visitation of His appearance and public ministry.[19] They were all alike given spiritual privileges. They saw the power of God at work. Yet they did not repent. And, in as far as they were deliberately rejecting the witness of God's Spirit, they were said by Jesus Himself to be committing sin of which there is no forgiveness.[20] As He plainly taught in the parable of the wicked husbandman, those who knowingly and deliberately reject God's one only beloved Son can expect nothing but judgment.[21]

---

[15] Jn. 10:28; cf. Phil. 1:6.
[16] Matt. 7:20.
[17] 1 Cor. 3:13–15.
[18] See Matt. 11:20–24.
[19] See Matt. 12:38–45.
[20] Matt. 12:31, 32.
[21] Mk. 12:6–9.

Similarly, at the time of the exodus of the Israelites from Egypt, the people all experienced God's mighty works. They all shared in the benefits of God's deliverance on the night of the Passover and in the crossing of the Red Sea. Yet, in the wilderness, when the personal heart attitude of every individual was put to the test, many hardened their hearts in unbelief. They resented God's dealings. They wished to turn back and return to Egypt. They became in spirit apostate. And so they came under final and irrevocable judgment. God swore in His wrath, *"They shall never enter my rest."*[22] *They were overthrown in the wilderness.*[23]

May not the writer of this epistle have likewise meant that not only his readers but also many others of their generation had lived through days of extraordinary divine visitation, the days of the ministry, death and resurrection of Jesus, the days of the pentecostal outpouring of God's Spirit, when witness to God's truth had been confirmed *by signs and wonders and various miracles and by gifts of the Holy Spirit?*[24] If, therefore, after enjoying such privileges, and by an act of considered judgment and deliberate choice, any then commit apostasy, and resist and reject the witness of God's Spirit, is it not understandable that such cannot be given even by God Himself any further opportunity to change their mind? It is impossible once again to bring them to the place where they can and ought to repent. Their only prospect is judgment at God's hands.

Grounds for Encouragement: 6:9-20

Since the peril of falling by the way and of proving both unfruitful and apostate is so real there is all the greater need of *strong encouragement to seize the hope set before us.*[25] Since some who have enjoyed such great spiritual privileges may nevertheless prove *worthless,* bearing only *thorns and thistles,*[26] we need substantial assurance to convince us and others that a divine work of salvation has truly begun in our lives, and that God will not fail to complete in us the work which He began.[27] Since also the full worth and crowning rewards of our faith in Christ still lie in the future, we need evidence or witness to encourage us to hold on in sure and

[22] 3:11.
[24] 2:4.
[26] 6:8.

[23] I Cor. 10:5.
[25] 6:18.
[27] See Phil. 1:6.

certain hope, and not to throw away our confidence and our expectation.[28] For if we look only at things seen and at things of the present it would be easy to be tempted to abandon our Christian confession. But, if we are rather by faith to reckon on the certainty and satisfying value of things unseen and of things still in the future, we need solid grounds for such assurance. For our encouragement this writer here mentions four.

The first ground for encouragement is the fruit of good works already to be seen in his readers' lives; the love, that is, which they showed for God's sake in serving the saints, as they still are doing.[29] This is one of the *better things that belong to salvation*.[30] This love is here described as shown to God's name.[31] "The saints" are recognized by them as members of God's family and treated with active affection and goodwill for God's sake. Such activity is objective evidence that they are themselves partakers of the divine nature, and that God's work of saving and transforming grace is operative in them.

The second ground of confidence and of consequent hope is the character of God Himself. He is "not unrighteous".[32] He does not forget His promises. He does not fail to reward those who have pursued His way in faith and obedience. It is, indeed, *impossible that God should prove false*.[33] For He cannot lie. He does not go back on His word. He is ever active to make it good.[34] So that we have in Him and in His declared purpose to bless us in Christ a sure ground of confident expectation. For He has made a promise to us just as He did to Abraham; and what He has promised He is certain to perform. We can, therefore, and we ought, in full assurance, to seize the hope thus set before us, and to find in Him a place of refuge and of safe anchorage.

The third ground for encouragement is provided in God's confirmation of His words of promise by His oath and covenant. "The significance of oath-taking one may learn from the common practice of men.[35] Its purpose is to put an end to all doubt or misgiving about a promise and to silence those who would gainsay its certainty. Its veracity and sure fulfilment are therefore confirmed by the most solemn of pledges. This commonly involves swearing by Almighty God. When men in this way pledge their word to one

[28] Cf. 10:35.   [29] See 6:10.   [30] 6:9.
[31] See 6:10, AV.   [32] 6:10 AV.   [33] 6:18.
[34] See Num. 23:19.   [35] See 6:16.

another they virtually call upon God Himself to mediate or stand
between them as a witness of their promises, and to watch over
their fulfilment of them.[36] As someone greater He is able to take
vengeance if either party fails to keep his word. This certainty of
divine vengeance makes swearing by God final as a way of confirming promises. In order to make men doubly sure of His promise
God has condescended to use this method of oath-taking.[37] So He
made Himself (since there was no one greater to appeal to) a kind of
third party or mediator between Himself and men. So we have a
double ground of confidence, in God the Promiser who gives us His
word and in God the Guarantor who confirms it by His oath. There
is therefore no possibility of being deceived or disappointed."[38]

This is how Abraham was encouraged to persist in hope through
a long period of waiting; and God's dealings with us in Christ are
similar. We, too, are called to be followers of *those who through
faith and patience inherit the promises.*[39]

The fourth ground of full assurance and great expectation is to
be found in Jesus Himself, already entered into God's presence and
permanently enthroned at His right hand. Here[40] the writer of the
epistle returns to his main theme, and to his concern to make
Christians aware of the importance for present Christian faith and
hope of grasping the truths concerning the Melchizedek order of
Christ's priesthood. For, as our high priest, Jesus has not only won
full entrance into the inner shrine of God's presence, but also He
there sits permanently enthroned as one who can never die or be
dislodged. Of this achievement the way in which an anchor functions is an apt symbol.[41] For an anchor penetrates unseen depths,
it becomes fixed or steadfast, and in this way it offers sure confidence and hope to those who hold on to it, and are held by it.
Similarly Jesus Himself has become our anchor and our hope.

What is more, Jesus entered God's presence not only *on our
behalf*, but also *as a forerunner.*[42] This means that He can be followed. He opened up the road for others to enter in. So we can
come where He is, to Jesus on the throne, and *seize the hope set
before us.*[43] For He is, too, not only the *pioneer* but also the *perfecter of our faith.* By holding on to Him, or rather as being held

[36] See Jdg. 11:10; Rom. 1:9.   [37] 6:17, 18.
[38] New Bible Commentary, p. 1099.   [39] 6:12.
[40] 6:20.   [41] 6:19.
[42] 6:20.   [43] 6:18.

firm by Him – as our anchor – we can be sure we will persevere to the end, and receive what has been promised.[44]

The Consequent Challenge: 6 : 11, 12

At this point the writer of the epistle shows his affection for his readers by addressing them (here only) as *"beloved"*.[45] What he asks from them is earnestness and diligence instead of sloth or sluggishness. They have shown that their new life in Christ is capable of such zeal in the love which they have displayed in ministering to their fellow-Christians. What he now presses upon them with great urgency is the need for them to put the same fervour and devotion into embracing, pursuing and, in God's time, possessing the hope set before them in Christ.

Enthusiasm is needed, he declares, on the part of each one of them *in realizing the full assurance of hope until the end*. For the greatest of God's promises are to be inherited only *through faith and patience*. We need to learn from those who have trodden this path ahead of us, and to *imitate their faith*.[46] Abraham is such an example. What he exhibited was "length of spirit" or, to coin a word, "longanimity". He was willing to wait, to hold on, to sustain pursuit, not to abandon hope or to give up expecting because fulfilment was long delayed. *And thus Abraham, having patiently endured, obtained the promise.*[47]

Similarly if we are to keep on keeping on in the present pathway of God's will and of faith's endurance, we need the inspiration of a God-given assurance of which no temporary delay, disappointment, distress or darkness can deprive us. Only so shall we go on with God to full maturity here and to a full entrance into the crowning glory hereafter. What we should be singing – and what should keep us singing "through the night of doubt and sorrow" – is "songs of expectation".

Such truth is for us the more timely because we live in a day when even Christians have largely ceased to be other-worldly and heavenly minded. Whereas the truth plainly revealed for our warning is that "If in this life only we have hope in Christ, we are of all men most miserable", or "to be pitied".[48] Rather therefore should

---

[44] See 2 : 10; 10 : 35, 36; 12 : 1, 2; cf. Phil. 1 : 6.
[45] 6 : 9.   [46] 13 : 7.   [47] 6 : 15.
[48] 1 Cor. 15 : 19 AV. and RSV.

we help one another to rejoice more in the certainties which are unseen, and to let our manner of life be increasingly determined by the goal in view over the horizon.

> "One the object of our journey,
>   One the faith which never tires,
> One the earnest looking forward,
>   One the hope our God inspires."

And we desire each one of you to show the same earnestness in realizing the full assurance of hope until the end, so that you may not be sluggish, but imitators of those who through faith and patience inherit the promises.[49]

[49] 6:11, 12.

Seven

The Better Promises of the Better Covenant

7:11, 12, 18, 19, 22; 8:6–13; 9:1, 9–22

IN BRINGING MEN INTO RELATION WITH HIMSELF GOD HAS BEEN pleased to pledge Himself in covenant. The covenant serves to establish and to seal the special relations between God and His chosen people. He thereby formally takes them to be His people and gives Himself to be their God. By its explicitly declared terms those, who thus become His people, enjoy special privileges and also become involved in corresponding obligations.[1]

The particular Greek word used to describe such a covenant is not the common word for a mutual contract in which two participants share equally. It denotes a disposition or undertaking made by one party or donor by which other parties may benefit on the conditions stated by the covenant-maker. This happens when a person makes a will, and so "will" or "testament" is a possible meaning of the word. "Covenant" is, however, in the scriptural usage a more appropriate translation, for it brings the participants – that is God and His people – into present and permanent living personal relationship in a way in which a will cannot do.

The First Covenant Failed: 7:18, 19; 8:7–9; 9:9–10

God first made a covenant with the Israelites *on the day when He took them by the hand to lead them out of the land of Egypt.*[2] This covenant was confirmed at Sinai and sealed by the sprinkling of blood, and by the acceptance by the Israelites of the divinely-declared conditions of benefit. *"All that the Lord has spoken"*, they affirmed, *"we will do, and we will be obedient".*[3]

This covenant failed to achieve full success for two reasons.

[1] See Gen. 17:7, 8; Exod. 19:4–6.
[2] 8:9; Cf. Exod. 6:4–8.
[3] Exod. 24:7, 8.

First, it depended for the fulfilment of its promises on men's performance of certain declared conditions – the observance of God's law or revealed will. These demands inevitably proved too exacting. So God said of the Israelites, "*They did not continue in my covenant*";[4] or "*. . . my covenant which they broke, though I was their husband.*"[5] Secondly, the ceremonies and sacrifices divinely instituted to provide atonement for sins committed, and to express a right spirit of penitence, faith and obedience towards God, while they had great symbolical value, had no essential moral worth. They could neither cleanse from defilement those who used them, nor create in them the will and the power to do God's will. *According to this arrangement, gifts and sacrifices are offered which cannot perfect the conscience of the worshipper.*[6]

So, as an institution or working arrangement the first covenant proved weak and useless. It *made nothing perfect*. It did not give men either full access to God's presence or full fitness for His company. In consequence it had to be *set aside* and a new and better arrangement introduced to take its place and to succeed where it had failed.[7]

Lest Jewish readers should understandably argue that a covenant divinely instituted could not thus be treated as of no use, the writer of the epistle is careful to show by quotation from the Old Testament that God's own attitude and intention in the matter had been clearly expressed long ago in a prophecy of Jeremiah's.[8]

Since God then spoke of making a new covenant with His people that implies that the first covenant cannot have been faultless.[9] Had it been, such a new covenant would not have been necessary. It implies also that its place in God's purposes was only temporary, and that it was meant to be superseded. Indeed, *in speaking of* the intended establishment of *a new covenant* he already *treats the first as obsolete. And what is becoming obsolete and growing old is ready to vanish away.*[10]

So we see that God's own word indicates that the first covenant must be regarded as having had its day and served its purpose. Men need and may look for the establishment by God of *a better covenant*[11] *enacted on better promises.*[12] There is hope for sinful

[4] 8:9.
[5] Jer. 31:32.
[6] 9:9.
[7] See 7:18, 19.
[8] 8:8—12 quoted from Jer. 31:31-34.
[9] 8:7, 8.
[10] 8:13.
[11] 7:22.
[12] 8:6.

men only if success is made to depend not on what men do to satisfy God, but on what God does to save and sanctify men.

A New and Better Covenant Established: 7:19, 22; 8:6–13

When the first covenant failed it was God Himself who saw the need of a better arrangement, and Himself promised in due time to provide it. *The days will come, says the Lord, when I will establish a new covenant with the house of Israel and with the house of Judah.*[13] It is in relation to, and in comparison with, the first covenant made at Sinai that this fresh covenant is described as second, new and better. Its introduction implies that the first is superseded and is to disappear.

The adjective here used for "new" means not just freshly made but also fresh and different in kind or quality. Because it provided in Christ's death a sacrifice which procured for sinful men actual redemption from sin's bondage, remission of sin's guilt, and purging from sin's defilement, it was calculated to succeed where the first covenant had failed. Also, its method of producing holy living was no longer external and legal; nor did it depend for its success on what men do to observe God's laws. Rather its method was spiritual and internal, and determined by what God can do to give men a new nature, and to work in them by His Spirit to cause them to will and to work to do what pleases Him.

Finally, as we shall consider more in detail later, because the Son of God is its Surety and Mediator, this covenant is eternal. It will never become old or obsolete. It will never need to be superseded. It guarantees full salvation for all for ever.

Its Ratification by Blood: 9:16–22

In Old Testament times and among the Hebrews there was a recognized ritual to be observed in connexion with the making of a covenant. It involved the introduction either of the blood or of the divided carcasses of slain animals; and the covenant-makers either had the blood sprinkled upon them[14] or themselves passed between the divided pieces.[15] The ritual thus used symbolized the violent death of the covenant-maker. By its introduction the covenant-

---

[13] 8:8 from Jer. 31:31.   [14] Exod. 24:7, 8.
[15] Jer. 34:18, 19.

maker visibly asked to be put violently to death if he told lies or failed to keep his word. He was thus swearing by his life. It was, it would appear, on such occasions that the phraseology was used, The Lord do so to me and more also if . . .[16]

So we are reminded by the writer of this epistle, *even the first covenant was not ratified without blood*. When its terms had been *declared by Moses to all the people, he took the blood of calves and goats . . . and sprinkled both the book itself and all the people saying, "This is the blood of the covenant which God commanded you."*[17] Also in 9:16, 17 the writer probably intends a reference to the familiar ritual of covenant making. If the word is translated "will" or "testament" the statements admittedly make sense in our world of thought; namely that the disposition of his property which a man ordains in his will, does not take effect until after his death. But the intended sense of the original Greek may rather be that where a covenant is involved the death of the one who is making it must "be brought"[18] in or symbolically introduced by means of the accustomed ritual. For a covenant takes effect, or is ratified and becomes operative, only "over the dead",[19] that is in the presence of animal corpses, which formally certify the covenant-maker to be as good as dead if he fails to keep his word thus pledged.

It is, too, in this very realm of thought and action that the second covenant is far superior to the first covenant. The ritual of the first covenant simply involved the covenant maker in liability to the death penalty if he failed to make good what it pledged; and the Israelites had thus failed to continue in God's covenant with them. So, far from it assuring them of blessing, it meant that they deserved to be put to death. In strong contrast to this the violent blood-shedding of Christ's death, by which the new covenant was inaugurated, was not a mere token or symbol of the penalty which would be exacted should there be failure, but it was itself a substantial sacrifice of infinite value. It was, therefore, adequate to provide redemption for all who were liable to the death penalty for transgressions under the first covenant.[20] It also provided from now on for all who come within its benefit actual moral purging of the defiled conscience, and consequent freedom to serve the living God.[21] Nor can they ever again be disqualified or declared liable to

[16] See Ruth. 1:17; 1 Sam. 3:17.   [17] 9:18–20.
[18] See 9:16, RV mg.   [19] See 9:17, RV mg.
[20] See 9:15.   [21] 9:14.

penalty because of sins they may yet commit, because the one sacrifice of Christ already offered is a sufficient substantial atonement for all the sins of God's people, past or future.

Here failure is impossible; and any further provision of necessary offering for sin, or any fresh exposure to the penalty of sin, are alike out of the question.[22] In Christ and through the covenant ratified by His blood both the redemption from sin and reception of the promised inheritance are alike eternal.[23]

Its Surety and Mediator: 7:22; 8:6; 9:15; 12:24

Of this new and better covenant Christ is both the Surety and the Mediator; and the ministry which he thus fulfils is, as we have already begun to see, much more excellent than any ministry fulfilled under the old covenant. A possible distinction between the two words which describe his work is to say that the surety pledges the fulfilment of an agreement, while the mediator negotiates or executes it.

It was by His death on the cross that Christ became *the surety of a better covenant*.[24] It was ratified by His blood. It is as the high priest on the throne, able to dispense benefits, that Jesus is *the mediator of a new covenant*.[25] It is to Him in the heavenly Jerusalem that we have and do repeatedly come for Him to fulfil His ministry as the mediator, and make ours the benefits which the new covenant promises. He is an all-competent minister; on the one hand, becaues of His once-for-all finished sacrifice,[26] and, on the other hand, because of His endless indissoluble life.[27] So He is able to complete to its full and final perfection the salvation of all who come to God through Him.

Its Better Promises and Consequent Benefits: 8:10–12

There are four blessings specifically guaranteed by the new covenant. These are: (1) God's laws are to be written on men's hearts. (2) Men are to know God as theirs, and to be owned as His. (3) Direct first-hand knowledge of God is to be personally enjoyed by every individual. (4) There will be complete and permanent remission of sins.

[22] 10:17, 18. [23] 9:12, 15. [24] 7:22.
[25] 12:24. [26] 10:10, 14. [27] 7:15, 16.

"If these four realities are reversed, it will be seen that they represent in the order of experience the four chief blessings of divine grace: (1) pardon; (2) fellowship; (3) consecration; (4) obedience."[28] Let us then seek to appreciate them in this reverse order.

(1) Verse 12. Our sins are fully forgiven and finally forgotten. They can never again be brought to remembrance and charged against us. Nor is continuance or repetition of offering for sin any longer necessary.[29] Indeed, it is wholly out of place. It is, too, through enjoyment of this amazing benefit that the distinctive evangelical experience of salvation in Christ begins. For by it we gain realized peace with God and freedom to devote our lives as a living sacrifice in His service.

(2) Verse 11. Each one of us may enjoy intimate knowledge of God as a precious personal experience. We have direct access to God; we may for ourselves each draw near to Him. We are no longer dependent upon a privileged class of priests to mediate between God and us. Rather as ourselves priests we may draw nigh, and, as no ordinary Levitical priest could do, enter the inner sanctuary of God's presence, there, not to be taught about Him by others, but to have the Lord Himself as our teacher, and to have Him making Himself known to us. Nor is this privilege in any way restricted to a select few or to the top ten. For from the least to the greatest all may know Him.

(3) Verse 10c. By the Lord's own covenant-seals and pledges granted to us individually as members of His people each one of us may be established in the amazing assurance that "I am His and He is mine." Just as a married woman has in the marriage service heard her beloved take her to be his, and has been allowed to take him to be hers, so we are meant to be assured that, in covenant bonds which can never be broken, we and the Lord who has made us His belong for ever to one another. This is an awareness that alters everything in life.

(4) Verse 10b. We may experience by the work of God's indwelling Spirit inner transformation of heart desire. God Himself will cause us to walk in His statutes.[30] We shall begin to have a new inner delight in the law of God.[31] We shall in some measure begin to make our own the testimony of the psalmist and above all of

---

[28] W. H. Griffith Thomas, *op. cit.*, p. 108.
[29] See 10 : 17, 18.   [30] See Ezek. 36 : 25–27.
[31] See Rom. 7 : 22.

God's Christ: *"I delight to do thy will, O my God; thy law is within my heart."*[32] This will make a new way of living not only possible but certain, by reason not of the forbidding external restraint of law but of the compelling inner constraint of life and love.

Thus full salvation can now be our experience. Because, by Christ crucified and enthroned, and by the blood of the eternal covenant, freedom from sin, fitness for God's presence, and full fellowship with God Himself are all made ours. These are the true ends of all religion and the declared object and goal of the covenant relation with Himself into which God in His grace has been pleased to bring us in Christ. No wonder that God's provision which makes such blessings ours is described as *a better covenant*[33] *enacted on better promises.*[34]

[32] Ps. 40:8.
[33] 7:22.
[34] 8:6.

Eight

A Single Sacrifice for Sins

9:1–10:18

Three Indispensable Requirements

GOD'S PURPOSE FOR MEN, AS EXPRESSED IN HIS COVENANT promises, and man's true destiny, as pursued in his religious activities, will find their fulfilment only as God and men become united in intimate fellowship. God and men must belong to, they must be possessed by, one another. As things are, however, man's sinfulness is a barrier to fulfilment. It separates men from God. It makes men unfit for God's company. It involves men in defilement and bondage and inevitable judgment. Consequently there are three indispensable requirements for the realization of God's purpose. These are, first, that men should be given full access to God's presence; second, that men should be made fit for His company; and third, that their sins should be dealt with once for all so that men will be troubled by their consequences no more.

The Inadequacy of the Old Jewish Ceremonies: 9:1–10; 10:1–4

While the Mosaic law recognized these requirements and indicated what was necessary to meet them, its forms and ceremonies were unable actually to achieve what they foreshadowed.

In the first place, as regards access to God *the first covenant had regulations for worship and an earthly sanctuary.*[1] These promised by their essential character the enjoyment of God's manifested presence, and the engagement by men in the activity of drawing near to Him. But, looked at more closely, they are seen to be unsubstantial and unsatisfying. For the sanctuary was earthly – *a copy and shadow of the heavenly sanctuary*[2] – a significant symbol but not the desired reality. *The Most High does not dwell in houses made with hands.*[3] Nor did its elaborate arrangements permit the

[1] 9:1.
[2] 8:5.
[3] Acts 7:48.

E

achievement by the worshippers of full personal access to God. For the people had to remain outside the tabernacle in the surrounding court. Into the outer tent only the priests – that is, a select minority – could go. Into the inner shrine only the high priest ever went, and he only *once a year, and not without taking blood*.[4] All this was an indication provided by the Holy Spirit Himself that *the way into the sanctuary is not yet opened*.[5] Put bluntly it symbolized the impossibility of full communion with God.

Nor in the second place, were the worshippers made by these ceremonies fit for God's company. *According to this arrangement, gifts and sacrifices are offered which cannot perfect the conscience of the worshipper*.[6] For since the *law has but a shadow of the good things to come instead of the true form of these realities, it can never, by the same sacrifices which are continually offered year after year, make perfect those who draw near*.[7]

Nor, again, in the third place, could the ceremonies set men free from the guilt and consequence of their sin. At its best the fitness thus gained was no more than a ceremonial *purification of the flesh*.[8] It was not a moral cleansing of the inner man. The worshippers still had a *consciousness of sin. For it is impossible that the blood of bulls and goats should take away sins*.[9]

Some truths carry with them very radical implications concerning the old Jewish ceremonies. It meant that, in spite of their divine origin and visible splendour, they were spiritually ineffective. It also meant that, while they had an instructive value as figuratively indicating what was necessary, they were obviously only a temporary provision *imposed until the time of reformation*[10] and intended to be superseded by substantial realities. So the realization of the very hopes towards which they pointed forward could but involve their complete abolition. Otherwise what was a God-given pointer to the truth of Christ might become an obstacle in the way of its full enjoyment. This, for instance was why Stephen, when he expounded the truth of Christ was rightly understood by his Jewish hearers to be speaking against the temple and the ceremonial law.[11]

[4] 9:7.
[6] 9:9.
[8] 9:13.
[10] 9:10.

[5] 9:8.
[7] 10:1.
[9] 10:2–4.
[11] See Acts 7:10–14.

The Efficacy of the Blood of Christ: 9 : 11–26

When Christ appeared as a high priest of the good things that have come,[12] then, by the sacrifice of Himself, He fulfilled – and thus made it possible for us to fulfil – the three indispensable requirements of realized fellowship with God. First, by His own blood – that is, in virtue of His sacrifice already offered – Christ gained once for all as our high priest decisive and permanent entrance into the very presence of God.[13] In consequence, the way stands open for us to draw near.[14] Second, because, as the sinless man, He offered Himself to God as a lamb without blemish, His blood – that is, the virtue of His sacrifice already offered – can purify our conscience from the defilement of our old sinful nature, and give us freedom to serve the living God.[15] Third, His death procured an eternal redemption for us.[16] The governing principle in relation to transgressions is that *without the shedding of blood there is no forgiveness of sins*.[17] His blood shed has ratified the new covenant. According to its promises God has declared, *"I will remember their sins and their misdeeds no more"*.[18] In other words, *by the sacrifice of Himself* Christ has *put away sin*.[19] So, what the old Jewish ceremonies failed to do, the blood of Christ has done and can do.

Because some modern commentators have tried to suggest that salvation by blood means salvation by participation in the life thus released and transmitted (as in blood transfusion), it is important to emphasize that, in the blood ritual of the Bible, blood is a token of blood shed in death.[20] It is not a means of sharing in life, but is evidence of life taken or sacrificed in violent death. It is evidence of the penalty of sin duly exacted and fully paid.

Also, because some contend that the slaying of the animal only released the blood, for atonement to be made by its subsequent offering in the sanctuary, it is equally important to emphasize that what is here said to procure remission of sins is the actual blood-shedding;[21] and that what is here said to redeem men from their transgressions is the death which has occurred.[22]

The Revised Standard Version is quite unjustified and very misleading in rendering 9 : 12 as *"He entered once for all into the Holy*

[12] 9 : 11.   [13] 9 : 12.   [14] See 10 : 19–22.
[15] 9 : 14.   [16] 9 : 12, 15.   [17] 9 : 22.
[18] 10 : 17.   [19] 9 : 26.
[20] See *The Meaning of the Word "Blood" in Scripture*, A. M. Stibbs, I.V.F.
[21] 9 : 22.   [22] 9 : 15.

Place taking not the blood of goats and calves but his own blood, thus securing an eternal redemption." For, in the original Greek, there is no verb indicating that He took His blood. Rather, it says, He entered "through"[23] His blood, that is, in virtue of His death or of His sacrifice already offered; and that He entered not in order to secure redemption, but as one who had already secured it.[24]

When the blood is subsequently said to be sprinkled this is done not in order to procure from God remission of sins, but in order to apply to individuals, who need it, the virtue of the sacrifice already made. This truth is plainly illustrated by the use of the ashes of a heifer mixed with water to procure ceremonial purification, and to sanctify for use in God's service.[25] For what was thus symbolically conveyed to the defiled person was not participation in the released life of the victim but a share in the virtue of its death.

In addition, we ought not to forget that the purification ritual of the old Jewish law was provided not to give outsiders initial entrance into membership of God's people, but to cleanse those who were already in covenant relation with God from freshly incurred defilement, in order that they might be ceremonially fit to enter God's sanctuary and to share in God's worship. Similarly, because those who have believed in Christ for forgiveness do not cease from sinning, we too need to learn how freshly incurred defilement may be cleansed. Otherwise such defilement can disqualify us both for fellowship with God and for the service of God.

What the Levitical ritual symbolically taught was that such defilement can be cleansed – and can only be cleansed – by the application of the virtue of a life laid down; that is, by blood shed and sprinkled. In addition, we are plainly taught here that this truth finds substantial fulfilment, and not just ceremonial counterpart, in the gospel of Christ. For the one sacrifice of Christ once offered has sufficient virtue to cover and cleanse, or put away, all the sins of God's people till the end of time; "till all the ransomed Church of God be saved to sin no more". What is more, the Christian fulfilment of the Levitical figures gives inner moral cleansing. The blood of Christ can purify your conscience from dead works.[26] The defiled, inhibited, shame-stricken sinner, paralysed by a deep sense of guilt is thus given new freedom of spirit to give himself without restraint to God's service.

[23] As is made clear by RSV mg.   [24] See 9:12 AV and RV.
[25] See 9:13; cf. Num. 19:17, 18.   [26] 9:14.

Unique Features of Christ's Sacrifice:
7:27; 8:2; 9:11, 12 (RV), 14, 23–26; 10:5–10, 14

Not only was Christ's work the true heavenly reality, of which the old Jewish ceremonies were only a temporary earthly figure, but also, because it was the heavenly reality, it possessed certain unique features which no earthly figure could possess. These features are noteworthy because they themselves mark the work of Christ as the true fulfilment of the anticipatory types or shadows, and give to His work its substantial and eternal worth.

First, then, let us notice that, as our high priest, in the necessary discharge of the work of offering a sacrifice for our sins, *He offered up Himself.*[27] He was at one and the same time both priest and victim. This was possible for Him for two reasons. On the one hand, as God incarnate He was both God and man. As God He could not die. For He was, as God, eternal or undying Spirit. It was as man that He suffered death. So, because still alive as God, in the moment of His death as man, He was able through *eternal Spirit* to offer Himself.[28]

On the other hand, as man He was sinless or *without blemish.*[29] No Levitical high priest could have offered Himself. Rather he needed to offer sacrifice *first for his own sins.*[30] But Jesus, being without sin, was able to offer Himself as the sacrifice for the sins of His people. So, while the Levitical high priest could enter the Holy Place only if he offered blood not his own,[31] Jesus entered for us through His own blood.[32] *He put away sin by the sacrifice of Himself.*[33]

Also, by Christ's offering, not of animals in ritual ceremony, but of His own body in moral obedience to God's will, a quality and value were given to His offering, which no animal sacrifice could possibly possess. This is the kind of offering which has successfully procured our salvation. *We have been consecrated through the offering of the body of Jesus Christ once for all.*[34]

In the second place, Christ as our high priest is *a minister in the sanctuary and the true tent which is set up not by men but by the Lord.*[35] He did His work of sacrifice and of winning entrance not in relation to an earthly man-made shrine in Jerusalem, but in relation

[27] 7:27.   [28] 9:14.   [29] 9:14.
[30] 7:27.   [31] 9:7, 25.   [32] 9:12, RV.
[33] 9:26.   [34] 10:10.   [35] 8:2.

to *the greater and more perfect tent (not made with hands, that
is, not of this creation).*[36] For while, in the fulfilment of the earthly
figure, it was ordained that the earthly copies of the heavenly
realities should be ceremonially purified with the rites of animal
sacrifices, *it was necessary . . . that the heavenly things themselves*
should be purified *with better sacrifices than these.*[37] So, through His
own blood, or by the sacrifice of Himself, *Christ has entered, not
into a sanctuary made with hands, a copy of the true one, but into
heaven itself, now to appear in the presence of God on our behalf.*[38]

This achievement outstandingly surpasses the best that could be
accomplished by the old Jewish ceremonies. For the Levitical high
priest only entered an earthly man-made shrine. In addition, he
went in hidden under a cloud of incense; and had very shortly to
come out again to spend the whole of the rest of the year outside.
In contrast to this Christ entered God's actual presence. Before
God's face He was, and is, openly manifested, as one who is wholly
acceptable in God's sight. And there He permanently abides *on our
behalf,* as our advocate with the Father; as the guarantor of our
access and acceptance; and as *a great priest over the house of God,*[39]
able to fulfil for all who come to God through Him the promises of
the new covenant.

Also, because Christ was acting throughout in relation to this
heavenly sanctuary of God's presence, it was at the moment of His
death on the cross, and not in some subsequent activity elsewhere,
that He successfully entered into the Holy Place. So, at this very
moment, outward earthly witness was borne to His achievement by
the rending in the temple of the excluding curtain.[40] It is from this
finished work of the offering of Himself on the cross, and in this
way entering for us once for all into the Holy Place, that all our
blessings flow. *For by a single offering he has perfected for all time
those who are sanctified.*[41]

Christ's Sacrifice: Its Finality: 7:27; 9:12, 25–28; 10:10–18

Christ's act of offering Himself for our sins was an act done once
and once for all. It achieved all that was necessary to procure man's
full and eternal salvation. He has no need to repeat His sacrifice,
like the Levitical high priests had continually to offer fresh sacrifices

[36] 9:11.   [37] 9:23.   [38] 9:24.
[39] 10:20.   [40] Mk. 15:37, 38.   [41] 10:14.

for sin both every year and every day. Nor is Christ, as some suggest, either eternally offering Himself to God in order to make atonement for our sins, or still offering up before God in heaven now the sacrifice or shed blood, which He is able to offer because of His death here on earth. Rather does the writer of this epistle repeatedly assert that the one event done in human history on earth, and in the flesh and blood of Christ's earthly body, fully and permanently secured for us an eternal redemption. For His act, though done in time "under Pontius Pilate", and outside the city of Jerusalem in Palestine, was an act done in relation to God and the heavenly sanctuary. By it, as our high priest, He won entrance for sinful men into God's presence. *He* thus *entered once for all into the Holy Place.*[42] Its consequences are eternal.

Let us notice with what insistence this truth is asserted in this epistle. In comparison with the Levitical high priests, we are told, *He has no need like those high priests, to offer sacrifices daily, first for his own sins and then for those of the people; he did this once for all when he offered up Himself.*[43] The force of this last simple statement is unmistakable. What needed to be done Christ did by one act once for all; and He did this when He offered up Himself; that is, in the event of His death on the cross, an event now past and finished.

Also, because the atoning work was thus achieved by earthly suffering, if any repetition were necessary, then repeated incarnations would be necessary, and they ought to have begun sooner in human history than the time of Christ's coming; and this plainly has not occurred. So on this point the writer of the epistle declares, *Nor was it to offer himself repeatedly, as the high priest enters the Holy Place yearly with blood not his own: for then he would have had to suffer repeatedly since the foundation of the world. But as it is, he has appeared once for all at the end of the age to put away sin by the sacrifice of himself.*[44]

This means that Christ's one incarnation and one death are sufficient and final in their consequence for all generations of men, past, present and future. Just as all men have but one earthly life; they live and die once, and according to the deeds done in the body in that one lifetime their eternal judgment will be settled, so Christ has by the deed done once and for all in His earthly body altered the eternal judgment otherwise bound to fall upon sinful men. For

[42] 9:12.   [43] 7:27.   [44] 9:25, 26.

in His body on the tree the penalty due to our sins has already been borne.[45] The offering necessary to bear our sins has already been made. So, when Christ re-appears at His second advent, it will be to complete our salvation. There will be no outstanding sin-question still to be settled. All this this writer asserts when he says, *And just as it is appointed for men to die once, and after that comes judgment, so Christ, having been offered once to bear the sins of many, will appear a second time, not to deal with sin but to save those who are eagerly waiting for him.*[46]

Twice later the writer of this epistle supplements this declaration on the positive side by declaring that, in accordance with God's will, Christ's one sacrifice already finished has secured permanently for ever both our setting apart to be God's and our corresponding perfection as His people. So he writes, *And by this* (i.e. God's) *will we have been sanctified through the offering of the body of Jesus Christ once for all.*[47] *For by a single offering he has perfected for all time those who are sanctified.* [48]

In further enforcement of this truth the writer of the epistle also contrasts the ineffectiveness of the Levitical sacrifices so endlessly repeated, all to no avail, with the complete success for all time of Christ's one offering already made and finished and divinely rewarded. So he writes, *And every priest stands daily at his service, offering repeatedly the same sacrifices, which can never take away sins. But when Christ had offered for all time a single sacrifice for sins, he sat down at the right hand of God, then to wait until his enemies be made a stool for his feet.*[49]

Since sin has thus already been put away by Christ's sacrifice, since by the shedding of His blood the new covenant has been ratified, since in this covenant God promises to remember our sins and misdeeds no more, any further repetition by Christ (or offering to God on earth by the Church) of Christ's atoning sacrifice is wholly out of place. For *where there is forgiveness of these* (i.e. our sins and misdeeds), *there is no longer any offering for sin.*[50]

---

[45] See 1 Pet. 2:24.   [46] 9:27, 28.   [47] 10:10.
[48] 10:14.   [49] 10:11–13.   [50] See 10:17, 18.

Other Outstanding Achievements

(i)
"Lo, I have come to do thy will, O God" (10 : 1–10)

In contrast to the unsatisfying ineffectiveness of the Levitical ritual Christ fulfilled the will of God. We are told here that, *He abolishes the first in order to establish the second.*[51] Let us consider what this means and implies.

In addition to the declaration that the Levitical sacrifices could never make perfect those who used them in order to draw near to God,[52] we are here confronted by the blunt and – as it may seem at first – the amazing statement that God did not want the animal sacrifices of the old Jewish ceremonies. It is significant that to express such an idea the writer of the epistle is able to quote from an Old Testament psalm. *Sacrifices and offerings thou has not desired. . . . in burnt-offerings and sin-offerings thou hast taken no pleasure.*[53] Inspired men of pre-Christian times had therefore already grasped this truth, that animal sacrifices are not what God really requires. They are, at their best, only figures of the true or *a shadow of the good things to come.*[54] They do not fully satisfy either God or man. Their only value is that they indicate what ought to be; and, since they were divinely ordained, to those who used them by faith, they were pledges of what God would provide. But that was all. They were not in themselves effectual as a sacrifice. *For it is impossible that the blood of bulls and goats should take away sins.*[55] God was not thereby fully pleased or satisfied. Nor was man's need actually met.

In contrast to this the truly satisfying activity, which animal sacrifies did but foreshadow, was the consecration to God's service of human lives. What God wants is the sacrifice not of animals but of human bodies, not something instead of man, but the man himself, with all his powers devoted to the doing of God's will. This is what pleases God.

So, when one came who said, *"Lo, I have come to do thy will, O God"*,[56] then the shadows and types were superseded. He took away the first when He established the second. For, as Samuel said long before, *"Has the Lord as great delight in burnt offerings and sacrifices, as in obeying the voice of the Lord? Behold, to obey is better*

[51] 10:9.   [52] 10:1, 4.   [53] 10:5, 6; from Ps. 40:6.
[54] 10:1.   [55] 10:4.   [56] 10:7.

than sacrifice, and to hearken than the fat of rams."[57] The Son of God became Man in order as man to do what men had failed to do – to please God. To this end God prepared for Him a body;[58] and with that human body He did the will of God. He became obedient to His Father's demands even to the extent of laying down His life. It is by His doing of God's will with His human body, in making it a sacrifice for our sins, that we are saved – sanctified and perfected for ever.[59] Consequently, while under the old law there was year after year regular remembrance of sin[60] and of the need of atonement, there is under the new covenant, and by its pledges of which we partake, remembrance of the one sacrifice which has put away sin.[61] By its promise we know that our sins are remembered no more.

Christ has also by His action as man revealed the character of true religion – the kind that really pleases God. He has left us an example to follow. From Him we learn that the way truly to serve God, and to offer acceptable sacrifice, is not by the performance of outward rites but by life devotion and heart obedience. On the one hand, the old ritual was the performance of an appointed form or ceremony. It could all too easily become the offering of something rather than the offering of self. On the other hand, the Christian religion is a way of moral obedience. It involves the personal choice of the will to do God's will. It involves offering of one's body as a living sacrifice.[62] This is the kind of worship that pleases God.

These truths can provide us with a practical test of our own Christian faith and practice. Does our hope of peace with God, of sins forgiven, depend upon the religious acts we repeat, or upon the finished act of obedience to God which Christ has already accomplished? Is our religion a sphere of endless uncertainty or a sphere of joyful assurance? Do we only hope some day to make good, or are we sure that, because of Christ's obedience to God's will – the offering of His body once for all – we are already sanctified and perfected for ever? Is our religion in consequence something outside ourselves – so many ceremonies to perform? or is it some One stirring us by His Spirit from inside? Is it a glad devotion of our bodies to do God's will? For it is Christ who by His coming changes

---

[57] 1 Sam. 15:22.   [58] See 10:5.   [59] See 10:10, 14, RV.
[60] 10:3.   [61] See Matt. 26:27, 28.
[62] See e.g. Rom. 12:1, 2; 1 Pet. 4:2.

one into the other. *He abolishes the first in order to establish the second.*[63]

(ii)

He sat down at the right hand of God (10 : 11–14)

By and because of His finished work of offering His one sacrifice of Himself, Christ has obtained from God the reward of permanent enthronement at God's right hand, and the promise that, in God's appointed time, fully realized triumph over all His enemies will be openly made His.

This is the chief theme and a crowning truth of this whole epistle. It is briefly summarized in its opening sentence, where the writer says of Christ that *when he had made purification for sins he sat down at the right hand of the Majesty on high.*[64] Nor is it merely the writer's own idea. He is able to quote from the Old Testament the prophetic word of the Father to the Christ : *"Sit at my right hand, till I make thy enemies a stool for thy feet."*[65]

The truth reappears in the writer's exposition of the fulfilment in Jesus of man's divinely-intended destiny. Concerning Him he says, *We see Jesus . . . crowned with glory and honour because of the suffering of death.*[66] The truth is reasserted as the chief point concerning Christ's priesthood. It is a feature that qualifies Him to save to the uttermost all who draw near to God through Him. So we read, *Now the point in what we are saying is this: we have such a high priest, one who is seated at the right hand of the throne of the Majesty in heaven.*[67]

In contrast to the negative statement "No cross, no crown" we see here the corresponding positive fulfilment. Of Jesus it can be said that He *for the joy that was set before him endured the cross, despising the shame, and is seated at the right hand of the throne of God.*[68] This is where by faith He is now to be seen. It is this vision of Him thus enthroned that can inspire our endurance, and assure us of perfection or salvation to the uttermost.

For His present position is a witness to three truths. First, the fact that He has taken His seat is witness that His work of offering sacrifice is already finished. This is in contrast to the Levitical priests, who continued to stand daily at their service, *offering repeatedly*

---

the same sacrifices, which can never take away sins.[69] In the second place, His position at the right hand of the throne of God is witness that power and sovereignty in and over the universe have openly been given to Him. In the third place, the words which the Father has spoken to Him concerning the future, and what He will do for Him, are guarantee that full victory over all His enemies is going to be openly realized. So He expects and awaits universal triumph.

It is to the throne of grace, where He sits, that we are in this epistle particularly exhorted *with confidence* to *draw near*, to *receive mercy and find grace to help in time of need.*[70]

The Confirming Witness of God's Spirit: 10:15–18

Nor is this confidence open to question. In order to make us still more sure we have added to the word of the Father, and the work of the Son, the confirming witness of the Spirit.[71] So *full assurance of faith,*[72] *the full assurance of hope until the end*[73] can be ours. More particularly, in the specific promises of the new covenant, promises whose original utterance the Spirit inspired, we are assured that God Himself will work in us to produce new desires to do His will, and that He will remember our sins against us no more.[74]

From these assurances two benefits flow. The holiness of changed conduct and of transformed behaviour becomes a practical possibility and a certain prospect. Also, we may be sure that no longer is there need or place for any engagement in atoning sacrifice or offering for sin; and all because Jesus, as our high priest, acting on our behalf, has offered one sacrifice for sins for ever.

[69] 10:11.   [70] 4:16.   [71] See 10:15–17.
[72] 10:22.   [73] 6:11.   [74] See 8:10–12.

Nine

The Alternatives Now Before Us

10:19–39

THE WRITER OF THIS EPISTLE HAS FINISHED HIS DOCTRINAL exposition. What remains to be done is to press home its practical application. The greatness of the blessings to be embraced, and the gravity of the peril to be avoided increase the writer's concern. At this stage of our study, therefore, we too must prepare ourselves to face and answer pointed demands for our active response.

The Pathway to be Pursued: 10:19–25

In this first relatively brief paragraph the writer summarizes the positive appeal of the whole epistle. As he had already shown in some detail, what makes new activities possible is first, Christ's accomplished work of atonement, and second, His continuing ministry in the sanctuary as the all-competent high priest of His people. He now demands of his readers that they – and, therefore, we – should actively give ourselves to these activities made possible for us by Christ; and, in particular, that we should give active expression to our Christian faith and hope and love.

In his concern to press this challenge home the writer of the epistle is not satisfied only to make brief demand for these activities to be engaged in. The lengthy sections which follow before the epistle ends are added to expand the treatment given to each activity; and to emphasize in turn the importance of the practice of these three Christian virtues. For faith, hope and love are, or ought to be, constant features of the life which we are henceforth called to live.

Possessions to be Used: 10:19–21

"Grace," writes Dr. W. H. Griffith-Thomas, "needs appropriation if it is to be operative. We see here, as before (in 4:14–16), the association of 'having' and 'let us'; because we possess, we ought to use and enjoy."[1]

First, then, let us notice what we now possess. Because of Christ's death for us the way into God's presence now stands permanently opened; and sinners such as we are can enter in with boldness – that is, both with heart confidence and active outspoken daring. When we do, we shall find Jesus within as the great priest over God's house, waiting to minister in God's presence to His people, and to make ours all the blessings of the new covenant.

It is well to pause, like the writer of the epistle briefly does, to appreciate the wonder and the cost of these privileges which are ours. Complete outsiders and unworthy sinners can now come right into God's presence. We were shut out by our sinful flesh, which deserved only God's judgment. The Son of God by becoming flesh – by being made sin for us[2] – and by offering His human body to be broken for us in sacrificial death, achieved, so to speak, the rending of the excluding curtain; and, by His blood, or through the virtue of His sacrificial death, opened a fresh and effective way into God's presence for us to tread. Indeed, the very way is *living* because Christ Himself is the way. No one comes to the Father, but by Him.[3]

The very same Jesus, alive and enthroned at God's right hand, is also the high priest who receives us when we do come to God through Him. He speaks to God on our behalf. It is His concern and ability to minister to all our needs as the mediator or executor of the new covenant. We have everything in having Him as our crucified and exalted Saviour. With such a high priest as ours, we can and we ought to have absolute confidence to enter the sanctuary of God's presence.

Practices to be Engaged in: 10:22–25

(i) *Let us draw near . . . in full assurance of faith.*[4] The first response to be made to the provision of God for us in Christ is the response of drawing near to God. This ought to become a frequently renewed activity, a regular habit, the way in which we consciously realize our fellowship with God in the sanctuary of His presence. This we may do with complete confidence, without hesitation or misgiving,

---

[1] "Let us go on", p. 134.   [2] See 2 Cor. 5:21.
[3] See Jn. 14:6.   [4] 10:22.

with no doubt or question concerning our right of access. This, therefore, we ought often to do expecting every time we draw near to obtain fresh mercy and grace to meet our need.

The full enjoyment of this way of blessing, henceforth always open before us, cannot however become ours in experience unless we fulfil certain obvious conditions of benefit. We must engage in such activity with complete sincerity of purpose. For God looks not at the outward appearance, but at the heart. Only the true in heart can know, and can continue to enjoy, the *full assurance of faith*.[5]

Also, every time we seek thus to draw near to God, we need afresh to recognize our need of present cleansing. Under the old Levitical ritual the high priest, before he could enter the sanctuary, had ceremonially to be made fit by the sprinkling of blood and by washing with pure water.[6] Similarly we can enter fully into our spiritual privileges in Christ only if we recognize our need of *clean hands and a pure heart*.[7] So we need to examine ourselves afresh on each occasion. We need to be willing to let God use His Word to convict us of sin and to make us clean.[8] We need, as we are con-victed, to seek fresh purging from inner defilement of mind and spirit. For when we are made aware of guilt, we can be set free to worship and to serve God in the liberty of the Spirit, only if *our hearts* are afresh *sprinkled clean from an evil conscience*. This Christ's blood already shed for us avails to do.

(ii) *Let us hold fast the confession of our hope without wavering*.[9] The full enjoyment of all that God has promised us in Christ cannot become ours here and now. The best is yet to be. The crowning consummation of our salvation still lies in the future. Because God, who has promised, is faithful and may be counted on to keep His word, our confidence is no vain hope or empty delusion. It holds in itself sure promise of *a great reward*. However, because we have to wait for fulfilment and meanwhile *do the will of God*, possibly by enduring trial or temporary darkness, it is of great practical im-portance that we should not abandon our hope and throw our confidence away.[10]

Such God-given hope is beginning to wane, and is likely to die, when those who possess it cease to glory and exult in it in out-spoken confession. Particularly should it be confessed before God,

[5] See 1 Sam. 16:7; Ps. 15:1, 2.   [7] See Ps. 24:3–6.
[6] See Exod. 29:4, 21; 30:20; 40:30–32; Lev. 8:6, 30.
[8] See Jn. 15:3.   [9] 10:23; cf. 10:35, 36.
[10] 10:35, 36.

and in the company of fellow-believers, in worship and song, in praise and prayer. *For we share in Christ, if only we hold our first confidence firm to the end.*[11] We ought to *hold fast our confidence and pride* (i.e. Gk. our glorying or boasting) *in our hope.*[12] So, says the writer again here, let nothing divert us from engaging in this activity. Let us see that we maintain the confession of our hope *without wavering.* Let us hold on to the faithfulness of God;[13] *for he who promised is faithful.*[14]

(iii) *Let us consider how to stir up one another to love and good works.*[15] We ought also to be giving expression to our new life in Christ in love and good works towards our fellow-men, particularly our fellow-Christians. To make sure that we do this to the full we ought to "provoke" or to "exasperate" one another. Here in the original Greek the attention of the readers is arrested by the use, with an obviously good meaning, of a word commonly used with a bad sense. What the writer implies is that in this sphere of activity we ought to set ourselves to find ways of stimulating one another to do the Christian thing, and to act towards others as true Christians should.

Since Christians thus clearly need to encourage one another, and the need for this will increase rather than decrease as the Day of the Lord gets nearer, it is of great practical importance that Christians should regularly meet together; and meet, as this exhortation implies, not only in the big congregation for acts of public worship, but also in additional meetings, which are small and informal enough for the detailed and sympathetic consideration of one another's personal circumstances and needs, and for every one present to share in giving as well as getting, so that all who come may gain from the mutual provocation and exhortation. Clearly Christians can be the best for God, and enter most into the possibilities of their new life in Christ, only if in intimate fellowship they actively help one another. Nor is it enough to know all this and to assent to it. Such practical instructions demand corresponding action. Nor is it difficult to begin. It can be done with two or three meeting in Christ's name – with the promised presence of Christ Himself in the midst of them.[16]

[11] 3:14.   [12] 3:6.
[13] See Mk. 11:22.   [14] 10:23.
[15] 10:24, 25.   [16] Matt. 18:20.

The Peril to be Avoided: 10:26–31

For those who are fully *enlightened*,[17] for those, that is, who by hearing and understanding the gospel have received *the knowledge of the truth*,[18] there are in the end only two possibilities. Either they can make wholehearted response to the gospel, and go on to Christian maturity through the steadfast expression of full devotion to Christ; or they can adopt an attitude of complete rejection, an attitude, that is, of absolute and defiant refusal, which must inevitably result in complete apostasy or abandonment of any acknowledgement of Jesus as the Christ.

It is this latter alarming possibility which is here described in its fully-developed form. As the writer of this epistle saw it, it was appropriate, indeed, it was urgent, that he should speak so bluntly and severely, because this very possibility of apostasy was for his readers an actual present peril, to whose dire character they needed awakening. We do well to remember that Scriptures such as this have been written to warn us also. Nor is such warning no longer needed. For we live in days when some, who have for years professed to be Christian, seem to be openly abandoning the faith.

If we put together in our thought the various references to this peril which occur throughout this epistle, we see that, as a wrong attitude, it begins with indifference and neglect, with failure to pay close attention to the message heard;[19] it develops into falling away and committing apostasy;[20] and it culminates in contempt and blasphemous defiance.[21]

One may compare with this two somewhat parallel Old Testament descriptions of progressive stages in religious decline; stages, that is, in man's departure from God and His truth. The writer of Psalm 1 indicates three activities which ought to be avoided by all who would experience blessing from God. These are walking *in the counsel of the wicked*, standing *in the way of sinners*, and sitting *in the seat of scoffers*.[22] Through the prophet Isaiah God said of His people, "*Sons have I reared and brought up, but they have rebelled against me. . . . They have forsaken the* LORD, *they have despised the Holy One of Israel, they are utterly estranged.*[23]

The kind of activity which is meant is described here in the

[17] 10:32.   [18] 10:26.   [19] See 2:1–3.
[20] See 3:12; 6:6.   [21] See 10:29.   [22] Ps. 1:1.
[23] Isa. 1:2, 4.

F

epistle to the Hebrews as sinning wilfully or *deliberately*;[24] that is, disobeying God-given witness to the truth by deliberate choice, by persistent attitude, by habitual practice. Its character is compared with, and in measure illustrated by, the man who "despised" or "set at nought Moses' law";[25] particularly, for instance, the man who, in the face of God's claim to exclusive worship, gave his religious devotion to other gods.[26] Two features here are noteworthy. First, it is significant that when a man thus sinned it was the responsibility of the community to bear witness against him and to inflict the penalty, and thus to put away the evil from their midst.[27] And, in the second place, the writer here explicitly suggests that the man, who similarly sins against the light of God given to us in Christ, deserves even worse punishment; and that this judgment the Lord Himself will execute.[28]

The kind of sinful activity which is here meant is next fully described in Christian terms, as doing open despite and flagrant dishonour to Christ's divine person, to His saving work and sanctifying blood, and to the gracious constraining Spirit of God. It means nothing less than defiantly trampling on the approaches of divine love. It means deliberately desecrating the sacred and outraging the Holy One. It seems comparable to what Jesus described as blasphemy against the Holy Spirit, of which He said there is no forgiveness.[29]

So, supposing any of us were to commit such sin (but note that the writer says only "if we do", not "because some have") the awful inevitable consequences are indicated. For such sin there is no atoning sacrifice. God has no second gospel in reserve for those who reject His one gospel. Such sin is without hope of remission. For such sinners there is not only no redemption but also no prospect but certain and the severest judgment. For they have God Himself active against them in holy wrath. During this life they have inescapably before them *a fearful prospect of judgment, and a fury of fire which will consume the adversaries*.[30] And in the coming Day it is God Himself whom they must encounter as their judge. *For we know him who said, "Vengeance is mine, I will repay". And again, "The Lord will judge his people". It is a fearful thing to fall into the hands of the living God*.[31]

---

[24] 10:26.
[25] 10:28, AV and RV.
[26] See Deut. 17:2–7.
[27] Cf. 1 Cor. 5:5, 13.
[28] 10:29, 30.
[29] Mk. 3:29.
[30] 10:27.
[31] 10:30, 31.

Encouragement to Keep On Believing: 10:32–39

Should any of us be thus tempted to abandon Christianity, to give up faith in Christ, and to cease to confess the Christian hope, let us find, as the first readers of this epistle were here exhorted to find, inspiration to keep on believing in two complementary ways – first, by looking back, and then, by looking forward.

By looking back to their own early experience as believers in Christ, these Christians were exhorted to learn from their own personal trials, and triumph, and testimony. For their own experience could serve to remind them that for Christians, who would be faithful to Christ, public exposure to *abuse and affliction*[32] is sometimes inevitable, either for themselves, or for fellow-Christians with whom it is their privilege to be associated. Also, the spirit in which they then triumphantly endured such trials could make them freshly aware that the pain and loss, which such persecution may involve, can be accepted with joy, when they are compared with the consequent and corresponding heavenly and eternal gain.

It may well be true that we, too, can and should find encouragement and challenge to sustained devotion in the same way – by looking back. For some features essential to Christian steadfastness are often early learnt in the experience of new converts, who quickly taste the meaning both of earthly sacrifice and heavenly joy. If such was to some degree once our experience, then, when we are now tempted to falter and to give up pursuing, we can and should find encouragement to continue, by recalling the enthusiasm and readiness to make sacrifice, which were characteristic of the first days or early years of our own Christian discipleship. Such memories should rebuke our present despondency and half-heartedness.

These Christians were also exhorted to find inspiration by looking forward in faith and hope; and by realizing afresh that such confidence in God as had become theirs is not misplaced. It holds sure promise of coming *great reward*;[33] and so it ought not to be foolishly thrown away.

Not only so; by heavenly and eternal standard the fulfilment will also soon take place. There is need to wait only *a little while*.[34] Then, not only will things long-expected happen, but also, and most decisively of all, Christ Himself will reappear to save.[35] His

[32] 10:33.   [33] 10:35.   [34] 10:37.
[35] Cf. 9:28.

promised personal advent is sure. So it is for us, as well as for those early Christians to live in the eager anticipation of Christ's coming and not to abandon faith and hope.

Meanwhile, in between today and the Day[36] of fulfilment, there are in God's will for us tasks to be done, and trials to be faced, all of which call for endurance and perseverance to the end. Only so can the full reward be possessed. *Therefore, do not throw away your confidence.*[37]

Possession or Perdition: 10:38, 39

Finally, there are, for all who know these things, only two possible alternatives; either to find acceptance with God and to inherit His promises by holding on in faith; or to withdraw one's confidence, to come under God's displeasure, and to perish by apostasy. The only alternative to complete abandonment to Christ is complete abandonment of Christ. There is, in the last analysis, no middle course.

For us, who have experienced in Christ God's saving grace and the work in us of His sanctifying Spirit, the latter course is surely unthinkable. No true Christian in his senses can seriously contemplate committing spiritual suicide. So, let us make the concluding choice and confession our own; that is, on the one hand, that *we are not of those who shrink back and are destroyed*; and, on the other hand, that we are, and intend to prove ourselves to be, *of those who have faith and keep their souls.*

What this last statement declares is that faith persisted in is the sufficient and indispensable principle not only of entrance into life but also of the full enjoyment of salvation. We are, or ought to be, those who believe unto "the gaining of the soul".[38] This means that we intend, as our Lord taught, to possess or win our souls, or gain our lives, through patience or endurance to the end.[39] This idiomatic phrase "to win our souls" obviously means to become the people that God intends us to be; that is, by the grace and work of God in creation and redemption, to become our true selves. This is where our true wealth for the future lies and ought to be sought. For, in the end, every man will either gain or lose himself.[40] So, in contrast

---

[36] See 10:25.   [37] 10:36.   [38] 10:39, RV mg.
[39] See Lk. 21:19, AV, RV and mg., RSV.
[40] See Lk. 9:24, 25.

to others who are not thus trusting in God and His faithfulness, we should live as those who know that we ourselves have *a better possession and an abiding one*;[41] or, perhaps even more significantly, as those who know that we are to have ourselves in true abiding self-possession. So may God help us to be *imitators of those who through faith and patience inherit the promises.*[42]

[41] 10:34; see RV mg.
[42] 6:12.

Ten

Living by Faith

Faith in God or outspoken confidence and hope in Christ is the principle not only of entrance into life, but also of its sustained, increasing and full enjoyment. This is what the writer of this epistle is most concerned to emphasize. If we are to reach spiritual maturity and fully to inherit God's promises we must have faith and patience; we must keep on believing.

Practical Value of the Old Testament: 11:1, 2, 4, 39

From the Old Testament we learn that under God's providence there has been a long historical sequence of individuals, who have acted and achieved, or waited and suffered, as men inspired by faith in God. These individuals, their attitude and actions, and their consequent experience and enrichment, provide substantial evidence concerning the character and the value of living by faith. What is more; because they thus pleased God, God has shown His approval of their conduct by having witness borne to them for the enlightenment and encouragement of others. So their doings as believers in God are recorded for our instruction; and in this way, although they are long since dead and gone, they still speak. They have a message for us to which we ought to give our attention.

How Faith Works: 11:1, 6, 7, 11, 13, 16, 24–27, 30, 35

Faith is distinctive in its activity. Particularly is it different from sight and from present sense observation and satisfaction. For it characteristically takes interest in the unseen and the future.[1] To the believer the supreme reality is God Himself; he thinks and acts and hopes *as seeing him who is invisible*.[2] To the believer life's greatest good is found in God's faithful activity on his behalf; in His fulfilment of His promises, and in His rewarding of seekers. Such fulfil-

[1] 11:1.   [2] 11:27.

ment is commonly a hope of the future rather than an observable fact of the present. What, therefore, faith provides is established conviction concerning things unseen, and settled expectation – a veritable "title-deed" – of coming future reward. Such faith inevitably influences a man's whole outlook and behaviour.

In the record of the individuals mentioned in this chapter the emphasis throughout is on these two things: on their awareness of unseen divine realities, and their assurance concerning future divine performance. Such conviction became theirs by faith, and was commonly in striking contrast both to visible appearances and to natural prospects. These men and women lived in the here and now of this life like "strangers and pilgrims".[3] They looked beyond present circumstances and experience, desiring *a better country, that is, a heavenly one.*[4] Beyond pain and suffering and death itself they expected to "obtain a better resurrection", and thus to *rise again to a better life.*[5]

Without faith it is impossible to please God. For whoever would draw near to God must believe that he exists and that he rewards those who seek him.[6] Faith's full activity is thus shown to involve a sequence of three complementary steps. It begins by believing that God is. It acknowledges the personal existence and the sovereign power of the unseen God. Next, it recognizes that He is the person above all others with whom it is desirable and most worth while to have personal dealings. For He is absolutely trustworthy. His gracious responsive action can always be counted on. *He rewards those who seek him.* Thirdly, and finally, therefore, full faith acts in the light of such awareness and conviction. It draws near to God in acknowledgement, in expectation, and in complete self-committal.

Such response of faith towards God is initial and basic. This is how faith begins. Faith then comes to complete expression and reveals its practical and steadfast continuance in three complementary kinds of activity. These are obedience, persistence and sacrifice.

First, true faith obeys God. It acts in the light of His word and in response to its demands. So Noah, out of reverence for a word from God which spoke of impending judgment, and which indicated the way to obtain deliverance, acted in obedience. Believing that what

[3] 11:13, AV.   [4] 11:16.   [5] 11:35, AV and RSV.
[6] 11:6.

God said would certainly be fulfilled, he *constructed an ark for the saving of his household*.[7] Let us notice here the explicit stress on the unseen and the future. The realities, which moved Noah to act in faith, were the unseen God and the coming judgment.

Second, true faith holds on. It persists in hope and in obedience. In spite of the natural unlikelihood or apparent impossibility of faith's expectation, and sometimes in the face of men's scorn and ridicule, it keeps on believing. It praises God in anticipation of coming fulfilment. This is how *Sarah herself received power to conceive, even when she was past the age, since she considered him faithful who had promised*.[8] This is why *the walls of Jericho fell down after they had – by faith – been encircled for seven days*.[9]

Third, true faith is so sure of God and His faithful fulfilment of His pledged word that it is ready to suffer rather than to disobey or be found false. So *by faith Moses . . . refused to be called the son of Pharaoh's daughter, choosing rather to share ill-treatment with the people of God*.[10] Under extreme pressure and violent persecution such faith is even ready to die rather than deny its confidence and its hope. So for their faith *some were tortured, refusing to accept release*.[11]

Faith in God thus transforms character. It inspires and sustains both action and passion, both achievement and endurance, both service and sacrifice. It enables men, or rather the God in whom they trust enables them, to become, to do, and to suffer the otherwise impossible; and thus to glorify God and themselves to find life in its fulness.

The Rewards of Faith: 11 : 3–7, 16

Let us consider one by one some of faith's rewards.

(1) *Understanding*. A consequence of faith, which is fundamental to all spiritual progress, is understanding. *By faith we understand*;[12] for we thus come by divine revelation to an awareness of truth otherwise unobtainable by human observation or imagination.[13] *By faith we understand that the world was created by the word of God*. Faith thus recognizes God and His word – that is, His declared will and command – as a sufficient explanation of all that exists in

---

[7] 11 :7.　　　　　　[8] 11 :11.　　　　　　[9] 11 :30.
[10] 11 :24, 25.　　　　[11] 11 :35.　　　　　[12] 11 :3.
[13] See 1 Cor. 2 :9, 10.

the world around us. Faith also finds in the revelation afforded by God's word authoritative guidance concerning the way to please Him. This is what Abel must have done.[14] His sacrifice was more acceptable than Cain's because he offered in God's way, not man's; in accordance, that is, with what God required. "As a result Abel is still speaking by telling of the necessity of blood-shedding for acceptance with God."[15]

(ii) *Pleasing God.* By their faith, first Abel in his act of worship, and later Enoch in his manner of life, both pleased God. *And without faith it is impossible to please him.*[16] This simple and all-embracing response of personal faith towards God is the one and only thing required on man's part to secure acceptance in God's sight. When men thus believe God, God owns them as His, and condescends to be known as theirs. *Therefore God is not ashamed to be called their God.*[17] So God called Himself, *The God of Abraham.*[18]

(iii) *Justification.* In God's sight the true believer is reckoned righteous. So, through his faith, Abel *received approval as righteous.* This is the witness that he had borne to him – that he was righteous, *God bearing witness by accepting his gifts.*[19] Similarly Noah *became an heir of the righteousness which comes by faith.*[20] Here the very phraseology indicates that his was no unique experience; and that "by faith" is a common and generally recognized way of acquiring righteousness. For what happened to Noah illustrates what in principle does or can happen to those who hear the gospel and believe it. For the gospel *is the power of God for salvation to every one who has faith. . . . For in it the righteousness of God is revealed through faith for faith; as it is written, "He who through faith is righteous shall live".*[21]

(iv) *Glorification.* Faith holds promise of glorification. This is the way to escape death and to be translated into a fuller enjoyment of God's presence. *By faith Enoch was taken up so that he should not see death; and he was not found, because God had taken him.*[22] So true believers do not go down into the darkness of the grave. Theirs is not the doom of a sinner's death. Rather they depart to be *at home with the Lord.*[23] Also, they may expect ultimately a share in

---

[14] 11:4.
[15] W. H. Griffiths Thomas, *"Let us go on"*, p. 151.
[16] 11:4–6.   [17] 11:16.   [18] Exod. 3:6, etc.
[19] 11:4, RSV and RV.   [20] 11:7.   [21] Rom. 1:16, 17
[22] 11:5.   [23] 2 Cor. 5:8.

that glorification of the whole man, body as well as soul, of which Enoch's physical disappearance was an earnest, and of which the empty tomb of the risen Lord is the final pledge.

(v) *Witness for God.* God is also pleased, as this very record demonstrates, to let believers in Himself, like Abel, Enoch and Noah, become examples and exhibits whose testimony he uses to encourage and instruct others to exercise similar faith in God. The story of their faith and its results has a message and a ministry. Such witness can issue, and it does issue – as in Noah's case – in both the salvation and the condemnation of others.[24]

Abraham's Faith: 11 : 8–12, 17–19

By faith Abraham obeyed when he was called to go out to a place which he was to receive as an inheritance; and he went out, not knowing where he was to go.[25] Abraham's faith was in a marked way the expression of a *conviction* concerning *things not seen* and of an assurance of things hoped for.[26] His faith was ready for venture into the new and the unknown. Abraham's obedience shows us faith on the move towards the possession of the promised inheritance. He staked his all on God and His faithfulness. He did this because *he was called*. He was a man to whom the word of God came – demanding obedience. His response was response to a person. He made the great decision to obey. He loosed his hold of the known and the visible, of present security; he counted on and anticipated unseen reward and future fulfilment, knowing for certain only one thing – the faithfulness of God. This was his simple and sufficient confidence.

By faith he sojourned in the land of promise, as in a foreign land, living in tents with Isaac and Jacob, heirs with him of the same promise.[27] In the quest of faith Abraham became a pilgrim. He was content temporarily to dwell like a stranger and a sojourner in a land not his own. He acted, that is, like a traveller on the road, anticipating a fulfilment lying over the horizon. So he lived in Canaan as if it were to him a foreign country, belonging to others; and he did this without losing heart or faith. Paradoxically the only settled dwelling which he had was a movable one – a tent. Such a

---

[24] Cf. Jn. 3 : 17, 18; 2 Cor. 2 : 14, 16.
[25] 11 : 8.   [26] 11 : 1.
[27] 11 : 9.

manner of life left him free at once to strike camp and go on with God.

We may well contrast with Abraham's spirit of true faith the way in which local churches, or Christians of long standing, too often lose this pilgrim attitude to life. Indeed, do we not all need to take heed? For history and experience indicate that it is all too easy to become excessively dependent upon elaborate earthly comforts and conveniences, to become tied to rigid and limiting institutionalism, to find that big church buildings have become more of a liability and a hindrance than an asset and an aid to progress. So, it is still appropriate for us to imitate the attitude of these ancient men of faith; that is, like them, ourselves to acknowledge that we are "strangers and pilgrims on the earth",[28] and to live accordingly.

In addition, it is noteworthy that, although Abraham had been promised by God Himself a settled dwelling place as an inheritance, Abraham made no self-willed attempt to hasten the accomplishment of God's promise. Nor did he abandon hope because fulfilment was long delayed. He was content to wait God's time and to keep His way.[29] Thus he learnt by faith to anticipate and to desire a better and a heavenly fulfilment.[30] *For he looked forward to the city which has foundations, whose builder and maker is God.*[31]

This last statement implies that Abraham looked not only for a place in which to dwell – *a homeland*[32] – but also, and still more, for a community to inhabit it. He looked for a city, not empty but fully populated, of which God, not he, was to be both the architect and the builder, the designer and the producer. In the Greek the word used to express the second of these ideas includes the suggestion that what is more important than the place to be inhabited is the creation of the people to call it their own. For it takes people, not merely walls, to make a true city.

Certainly the full faith of Abraham included both expectations; that God would provide both a country to be inhabited and a people to inhabit it. The city and the community here ultimately in view are obviously the heavenly Jerusalem, of which, as "the mother of us all",[33] all who are Christ's are privileged to be citizens. As, therefore, we may learn from Abraham to anticipate by faith our heavenly inheritance, the city which God has prepared for His

[28] 11:3, AV.; cf. 1 Pet. 2:11.   [29] See Ps. 37:34.
[30] 11:16.   [31] 11:10.   [32] 11:14.
[33] Gal. 4:26, AV.

people, we should also learn from Abraham to trust God to prepare
us to be worthy of our inheritance; and also to make up the number
of His elect, in order to hasten the day of fulfilment, when the completed city can be finally revealed and enjoyed.[34] *For here we have
no lasting city, but we seek the city which is to come.*[35]

*By faith Sarah herself received power to conceive, even when
she was past the age, since she considered him faithful who had
promised.*[36] It is at this point in the outworking of God's purpose to
bless Abraham that Sarah finds her place. For her participation was
necessary to the birth of the descendants of Abraham who were to
possess the promised inheritance. Sarah, too, had faith to embrace
the realities of the unseen and the future. She counted on the God
of the promise and on His faithful doing in fulfilment of His word.
She expected herself to give birth to a man child, and thus to found
a "seed" or family which would continue and increase. Such a
record outstandingly illustrates the truth that men called to God's
service who are married, cannot become the best for God without
the believing co-operation and personal consecration of their wives.
It is sad, indeed, if, for lack of faith, the woman in such a partner-
ship turns down a divinely-inspired proposal, as Sarah might so
easily have done, as naturally impossible.

When at their age, God promised a son to Abraham and Sarah
their first reaction was one of incredulous laughter.[37] The very idea
seemed ridiculous and out of the question. But, by God's grace, both
individually and together they rose to believing that God could and
would do for them what was otherwise naturally impossible. By
simply looking to God, and reckoning on His faithfulness, their faith
flourished and triumphed in circumstances of extreme natural im-
probability and hopelessness.

Also, such a victory "by faith" issued for them, as it still may for
us, in the most far-reaching consequences. *Therefore*, adds the writer
here, *from one man, and him as good as dead, were born descendants
as many as the stars of heaven and as the innumerable grains of sand
by the seashore.*[38] For the principle operative here is not merely one
of simple and limited addition but one of endless compound multi-
plication. It was such a fulfilment that Abraham's faith had embraced when God said to him, *"So shall your descendants be."*[39]

---

[34] See Rev. 21 : 2 – 22 : 5.   [35] 13 : 14.   [36] 11 : 11.
[37] See Gen. 17 : 17; 18 : 10–15; 21 : 6.   [38] 11 : 12.
[39] See Gen. 15 : 5, 6; Rom. 4 : 18.

By faith Abraham, when he was tested, offered up Isaac, and he who had received the promises was ready to offer up his only son, of whom it was said, "Through Isaac shall your posterity be named." He considered that God was able to raise men even from the dead; hence, figuratively speaking, he did receive him back.[40] Abraham's faith finally triumphed in the sacrifice of Isaac. Here he expressed his faith by no mere theoretical assent but in costly obedience, in readiness to sacrifice his dearest, in willingness to accept as right, because God demanded it, a course of action which he could not understand, and which threatened to put an end to all his hopes.

The most outstanding reaction of Abraham's faith to this searching test is seen in his refusal to see inconsistency or faithlessness in God. True, to human reckoning, the demand to sacrifice Isaac seemed a denial of all that God had promised. For, if Isaac were put to death now, how could he continue the family line, and be the father of the promised descendants? Abraham, however, simply believed that, since God had so promised, He could and would Himself resolve the problem thus created. Indeed, by faith Abraham anticipated and embraced God's way of doing this. *He considered that God was able to raise men even from the dead*. Had God not already in the birth of Isaac brought life out of death?[41] So Abraham daringly entertained by faith the hope of resurrection. He thus turned what would otherwise have been a way of darkness and a depressing dead end into a pathway of hope where God would significantly intervene in triumph as over death itself.

Faith's Hope Beyond Death: 11:13–16, 20–22, 35–38

These all died in faith. Men like Abraham, who by faith had an awareness of the unseen and the future, understandably came to believe that the complete and crowning fulfilment of hope could not be realized in the here and now of present earthly experience, and lay beyond death itself, and in heaven. So they believed not only that God could raise from the dead, and restore men to life here on earth; they also came to believe in "a better resurrection" and in *a better life* in the life beyond.[42] So, though they died, they did not die in the darkness of disappointment, but in faith and in the

[40] 11:17–19.   [41] See 11:12.
[42] See 11:35, AV and RSV.

anticipation of hope, with the light of a dawning day upon their faces. Thus they hailed the coming fulfilment beforehand, *not having received what was promised, but having seen it and greeted it from afar*,[43] like men journeying homewards, and not belonging, or wishing to take up settled abode here. Such faith made them acknowledge that they were strangers and exiles on the earth. And, adds this writer about them, *people who speak thus make it clear that they are seeking a homeland*.[44]

Also, they were so sure of the reward over the horizon that they resisted the temptation to go back. It never, indeed, entered their mind to discover or devise an opportunity to withdraw. They were no longer *thinking of that land from which they had gone out* with a kind of home-sick longing to return. Rather they acted as men who had set their mind and affection and all their desire on better and heavenly things, which were in due time to be enjoyed in fulfilment of God's promise. Nor was this a vain hope or a misplaced confidence. Rather they proved God's faithfulness as One always ready to be openly invoked as theirs; and their faith gave them the full assurance that He had already prepared for them a dwelling place.[45]

Such men of faith still have much to teach us. For it is still all too easy to be tempted to count our treasure and security and reward in things seen and present. Yet "if it is for this life only that Christ has given us hope, we of all men are most to be pitied".[46] The best is yet to be. The true fulfilment of Christian hope lies beyond our present experience.

By faith Isaac invoked future blessings on Jacob and Esau. By faith Jacob, when dying, blessed each of the sons of Joseph, bowing in worship over the head of his staff. By faith Joseph, at the end of his life, made mention of the exodus of the Israelites and gave directions concerning his burial.[47]

Isaac, Jacob and Joseph were all so aware of God, and so sure of certain fulfilment of His promises, that they looked beyond their own deaths, and anticipated future blessings for their children. Isaac, too, in submission to God's will, accepted that Jacob should come before Esau in blessing. Jacob gave to Joseph, who was not his eldest son, the double portion of the first-born, and blessed both of his sons. Joseph anticipated the exodus of the Israelites from Egypt,

[43] 11:13.   [44] 11:13, 14.   [45] See 11:15, 16.
[46] 1 Cor. 15:19, NEB.   [47] 11:20–22.

and refused to believe that he must be buried in Egypt. In each case, as what is said of them here explicitly emphasizes, these three men exercised faith concerning the future when their own deaths were very near. So they died in faith.

Some were tortured, refusing to accept release, that they might rise again to a better life. Others suffered mocking and scourging, and even chains and imprisonment. They were stoned, they were sawn in two, they were killed with the sword; . . . of whom the world was not worthy.[48]

Similar faith in a fuller life and in satisfying reward beyond death was supremely shown by the martyrs; by those, that is, who suffered greatly, and died painful and shameful deaths, rather than deny their faith or be false to the worship of the true God. Such men deserved something better than this fallen and sinful world has to offer or can provide. Nor are they to be disappointed. Their reward, as their faith rightly anticipated, will be a better life in the world beyond.

The Faith of Moses: 11:23–28

Moses and his story provide an outstanding illustration of living by faith. The source and inspiration of his faith are to be found in the close intimacy of his personal communion with God. Let us notice at once in the record here the explicit mention of his awareness of the unseen and his assurance concerning the future. *For he endured as seeing him who is invisible;*[49] and *he looked to the reward* – "his eyes were fixed upon the coming day of recompense".[50]

By faith Moses, when he was born, was hid for three months by his parents, because they saw that the child was beautiful; and they were not afraid of the king's edict.[51] Faith in God was found first in Moses' parents. He had the advantage of being born into a truly godly home, a home where there was faith not fear, hope not despair. His parents believed that God who had given them such a child must intend the child to live. They refused to accept the prospect that he must die. The royal edict did not fill them with alarm and apprehension. They trusted in God to preserve. Nor were they disappointed.

By faith, Moses, when he was grown up, refused to be called the

48 11:35–38.   49 11:27.
50 11:26, RSV and NEB. 51 11:23.

son of Pharaoh's daughter, choosing rather to share ill-treatment with the people of God than to enjoy the fleeting pleasures of sin.[52] Under God's providence, and by men's natural reckoning, Moses became in Egypt a man of culture and education with the status of a prince of the royal house. By contrast, the Israelites were in Egyptian eyes a despicable horde of illiterate slaves. Also, they were suffering oppression at the hands of the very world which was giving Moses wealth, comfort and privilege. Yet the unalterable truth remained that by birth Moses was an Irsaelite not an Egyptian. Also, *by faith* he was enabled to see the Israelites as *the people of God*, and, therefore, as the people of destiny, the people with a greater future before them than the Egyptians in the purposes of God. So Moses made his choice to throw in his lot with them, no matter what the cost and the consequent suffering. What is more, by faith he now saw the continued enjoyment of Egypt's natural attractions as "sin", as "missing the mark" of God's intended purpose for his life, and as "apostasy", that is a complete disowning, not only of the Israelites as his brethren, but also of their God as his God. So *by faith he refused . . . choosing rather*. There are circumstances, particularly sometimes in the lives of young people with life before them, where similar decisive and costly choice may still be called for. Any who are faced with the challenge to make such a decision should learn from Moses to have "respect unto the recompense of the reward".[53]

He considered abuse suffered for the Christ greater wealth than the treasures of Egypt, for he looked to the reward.[54] Moses faced the inescapable truth that to accept the call of God to such service of his brethren would involve affliction and reproach. But by faith he discerned the true character of such hardship as suffering for God and His Christ By faith he looked beyond the pain and loss to the consequent abiding reward. He looked, that is, as in the New Testament believers in Christ are explicitly encouraged to do at the unseen not the seen, at the eternal not the transient. By faith Moses discerned what Paul explicitly declares; that *this slight momentary affliction is preparing for us an eternal weight of glory beyond all comparison.*[55]

By faith he left Egypt, not being afraid of the anger of the king.[56] Moses thus dared to believe, in the face of the might of Egypt, and

[52] 11:24, 25.   [53] 11:26, AV.   [54] 11:26.
[55] See 2 Cor. 4:17, 18.   [56] 11:27.

the unwillingness of Pharaoh, which alike seemed to make it impossible, that, without any compromise or half-measures, God intended His people to quit Egypt, and not to be terrified into disobedience to God's will by Pharoah's power and wrath. So he repeatedly confronted an unwilling Pharaoh with God's unchanging demand: *Let my people go.*[57] So he withstood every suggestion of compromise. So he expected God to take them out safely, and to overthrow the Egyptians.

By faith he kept the Passover and sprinkled the blood, so that the Destroyer of the first-born might not touch them.[58] Moses believed that God's judgment was to fall on all the first-born in Egypt. He also believed that under the shelter of shed blood, in accordance with God's revealed will and provision, God would save His people from the judgment. What is clearly suggested here is that it was Moses' personal faith in God that moved the people to treat the warning of impending judgment seriously, and to appropriate for themselves the promised deliverance by the sprinkling of the blood of a lamb slain as a sacrifice. This suggests that hearers of God's word may sometimes be moved to believe and to obey the gospel by the faith of the preacher. For, in such preaching, as Paul declares, *the righteousness of God is revealed through faith for faith*; or "by faith unto faith".[59]

By faith the people crossed the Red Sea as if on dry land.[60] Thus did the personal faith of Moses become the public faith of the community. The people dared to make the venture of obedience and to go *into the midst of the sea on dry ground.*[61] Responding to Moses' lead, and counting on God's providential intervention, they achieved the impossible. *But the Egyptians, when they attempted to do the same, were drowned.*[62]

Victory by Faith: 11:29-35

So, as we have just seen, both in the deliverance of God's people, and in the frustration and overthrow of their enemies, indeed, no matter in what circumstances and necessity, *this is the victory that overcomes the world, our faith.*[63] In particular, let us learn from the way in which *the walls of Jericho fell down after they had been*

[57] See Exod. 5:1; 7:16; 8:1, 20; 9:1, 13; 10:3.
[58] 11:28. [59] Rom. 1:17; RSV and RV.
[60] 11:29. [61] Exod. 14:21, 22. [62] 11:29.
[63] 1 Jn. 5:4.

G

encircled for seven days,[64] that such faith must co-operate with God by acting in obedience to His word, and by holding on till His time is fulfilled. Let us learn from the way in which *Rahab the harlot did not perish with those who were disobedient* – for "by faith" she "escaped the doom of the unbelievers"[65] – that by such faith the outsider and the sinner may experience God's salvation, provided he will similarly change sides, and commit himself to God's mercy. Finally, as the record of many others and their deeds makes plain, let us learn that by similar faith victories of all kinds have been achieved – material, moral, and spiritual victories alike – culminating in receiving back the dead raised to life again, and in final personal victory over death itself.[66]

The Promised Reward: 11 : 39, 40

For all the sincerity and steadfastness of their faith in God, these spiritual pilgrims and warriors and martyrs of Old Testament times never fully enjoyed the promised reward. Indeed, it could not be enjoyed until, *when the time had fully come, God sent forth his Son.*[67] So *all these, though well attested by their faith, did not receive what was promised, since God had foreseen something better for us, that apart from us they should not be made perfect.*[68]

This means that, under God's providence, our lot is better than theirs, and fulfilment of God's promises which they only anticipated we can now actually experience and share in. Not that they are to be left out of this enjoyment. Rather in the coming day of resurrection and full salvation, when Christ *will appear a second time,*[69] we and they are to reach our perfection together.

[64] 11 : 30.
[66] 11 : 32—35.
[68] 11 : 39, 40.

[65] 11—31, RSV and NEB.
[67] Gal. 4 : 4.
[69] 9 : 28.

Eleven

Steadfast in Hope

12 : 1–29

FAITH, AS WE HAVE SEEN, IS FUNDAMENTAL TO ALL SPIRITUAL LIFE and progress. Without faith we cannot please God; nor can we inherit His promises. Such faith, if it is fully to possess what God has promised, must persist to the end. One compelling factor which should inspire such endurance is the sure hope to which the promises of God give birth. True faith is, because of this, *the assurance of things hoped for*.[1] What we must do is by faith to embrace the hope which God's promises set before us; and to hold fast to its confession without wavering, because *he who promised is faithful*.[2] It is to such steadfastness in hope that the writer of this epistle next exhorts his readers.

The Race Set Before Us: 12 : 1–4, 7, 12

Christians may profitably think of themselves as men involved in running a race. Here, what is important is to distinguish carefully the kind of race in which we are involved, and the qualities which successful participation in it demands.

First, we ought not to think of ourselves as all running the same course in competition with one another. For in Christian life and service each runner has his own course to pursue. In consequence, the proper goal of Christian endeavour is not to seek to outdo one's brethren, or to copy their achievements, but to finish one's own particular course. Two illustrations of this truth are to be found in the Acts. Paul once spoke of John the Baptist as *finishing his course*.[3] Also, when Paul himself was confronted by the witness of the Spirit that imprisonment and afflictions awaited him, his concern was, no matter what it cost, to *"accomplish my course"*.[4] This, therefore, ought to be the concern of every Christian – to pursue to the end his own divinely-appointed course.

[1] 11 : 1.
[2] 10 : 23.
[3] See Acts 13 : 25.
[4] See Acts 20 : 22–24; cf. 2 Tim. 4 : 7.

Second, the quality most demanded for the fulfilment of such an ambition is "endurance" or *perseverance*.[5] For the Christian race is not like a short flat race, but rather like a long-distance, cross-country, or obstacle race – a deliberately planned endurance test. It demands not brilliant starters or impressive sprinters but plodding stickers. For it is an all-life contest, and a test of staying power. Consequently, in this passage, the repeated emphasis is on endurance. We are reminded that Jesus *endured the cross*; that He *endured from sinners such hostility against himself*; and that *it is for discipline that you have to endure*.[6] What is of outstanding practical importance is *not to grow weary or fainthearted*.[7]

Such exhortation was obviously particularly needed by these readers. They were, it would appear, as Christians disappointed; beset by despondency and by the temptation to abandon the faith. They were certainly not going all out. So they are exhorted to pull themselves together, to brace themselves to fresh effort. *Therefore lift your drooping hands and strengthen your weak knees*.[8] Nor should we overlook the possibility that we, too, may ourselves need to heed this very word.

Inspiration to Endure: 12 : 1–10

The writer not only exhorts his readers; he also sets himself to inspire them by direct appeal to objective evidences which will encourage them to be steadfast. These same evidences can also serve to encourage us.

First, *we are surrounded by so great a cloud of witnesses*.[9] The appeal here is to the heroes of faith in Old Testament times, whose achievements have been recalled in the previous chapter. They are not to be thought of just as spectators. Rather they are runners of the past who have finished their courses. They are individuals with a witness or testimony to give. The writer of this epistle is thus exhorting his readers to find inspiration to persevere in the example and achievements of those who, in the past, have been successful in this very way. The record of their doings confirms that endurance is necessary, and shows that it is abundantly worth while. It issues in *great reward*.[10]

Secondly, the supreme example is provided by *Jesus* Himself and

---

[5] 12 : 1, AV and RSV.   [6] 12 : 2, 3, 7.   [7] 12 : 3.
[8] 12 : 12.   [9] 12 : 1.   [10] See 10 : 35, 36.

by His earthly career as a man among men. For He, too, finished His course; and, in order to do so, He *endured the cross, despising the shame*.[11] In order to complete His appointed task and path He preferred obedience to self-pleasing. He thus did God's will. In His struggle against sin, and against the temptation to withdraw from the divinely-appointed way, He resisted to the point of shedding His blood.[12] Through and beyond it all He anticipated the reward – *the joy that was set before him*.[13] He was steadfast in hope.

So it is for us, as each of us runs his course, to do so *looking* away *to Jesus . . . seated at the right hand of the throne of God*.[14] For in this whole sphere of faith's obedience, He is, to begin with, *the pioneer of our faith*, who has opened a way through for us to follow; and finally, He is *the perfecter of our faith*, who is able, as we trust Him, to make perfect unto the end – or to bring to its completion – the work of grace in us which He has begun.[15]

Thirdly, to inspire endurance there is the encouragement provided by the Scriptures. God's words *written in former days* were indeed written for this very purpose – *for our instruction, that by steadfastness and by the encouragement of the scriptures we might have hope*.[16] It is noteworthy here[17] that words from the Old Testament are treated as the voice of God conversing with men.

Fourthly, we need to appreciate that endurance has a worthwhile purpose. For God in causing us to pass through experiences which demand submission and perseverance is dealing with us for our discipline and growth in holiness. His purpose is to make us to *share his holiness*.[18]

Right Attitude of Heart: 12 : 1, 5–13

If we are to submit to discipline, and are not to become resentful or rebellious when thus treated, everything depends upon a right attitude of heart. We need an awareness that, in thus ordering our way, God is acting as a loving Father, and treating us as His children. Such treatment at His hands is to be regarded as nothing less than a proof of our sonship. It is individuals who lack such experiences who may question whether they are really true children of God at all.[19]

[11] 12 : 2.   [12] See 12 : 4.   [13] 12 : 2.
[14] 12 : 2.   [15] See Phil. 1 : 6.   [16] Rom. 15 : 4.
[17] 12 : 5, 6.   [18] 12 : 10.   [19] 12 : 5–8.

Consequently we should look beyond the circumstances which we have to endure, and beyond the "second causes" whose helpless and even unfair victims we may appear to be, to the sovereign God whose mind and hand control our affairs. Instead of resentfully resigning ourselves to our unwelcome lot, we should seek positively to be in willing subjection to our Father, and we should be actively concerned to share in the furtherance of His purpose for our good.[20]

So we should give Him our active co-operation. We should be willing for His discipline of us to do its work. We should be prepared to be "exercised thereby" or *trained* by the experience; knowing that, if God is ordering it for our good, what at the moment inevitably *seems painful rather than pleasant* will *later* yield worthwhile benefit for our enrichment.[21]

So we should refuse to let depression get us down. Rather we should be moved to responsive action by a sense of urgency and need; realizing that if the condition in which we are is not remedied, and that without delay, it may become worse and past remedy; like a lame leg which, if it is not treated and healed, may be put out of joint and become unusable and useless, indeed, a hindrance to progress.[22]

So let us face, and face at once, the challenge to be all out for Christ, the challenge to give ourselves to running the race that is set before us. Let us face the practical and personal cost of such all-out devotion. *Let us . . . lay aside every weight and sin which clings so closely*.[23] This means that we must be ready to cut out from our lives things which militate against effective spiritual progress; like a runner reducing his weight or his encumbrances in order to be able to run faster, or to keep going at all. What the Christian race demands is perseverance unto the end.

Perils Which Still Beset Us: 12 : 12–17

Once again this writer is impelled explicitly to warn his readers of dire spiritual perils – perils to which they are the more exposed because of their half-heartedness and lack of active enthusiasm in Christian discipleship.

He is aware that some of them are spiritually "lame". Such phraseology was used by Elijah to rebuke the people of his day,

---

[20] 12 : 9, 10.   [21] 12 : 11, AV. and RSV.
[22] See 12 : 13.   [23] 12 : 1.

when he asked, *"How long will you go limping with two different opinions? If the* LORD *is God, follow him; but if Baal, then follow him".*[24] The probability is therefore that what is being referred to here is a state of hesitation and indecision between full adherence to Jesus as the Christ or promised Messiah and attempted return to Judaism. They are in imminent danger of complete apostasy from Christ and abandonment of faith in the gospel.

The warning given is, in consequence, once again of the most blunt and severe kind; and the character of the danger is made more explicit by a threefold description. First, there is the peril lest any one of their number *fail to obtain the grace of God*.[25] The idea here is that of "falling out", or "failing to keep up with" a company on the move. The fear is lest, in a day of grace and salvation, when God is active to save, and they have heard in Christ His call to follow and to inherit God's promises any should by their own folly be left out of the enjoyment of God's blessing.[26]

Secondly, there is the peril lest a *"root of bitterness" spring up and cause trouble, and by it the many become defiled*.[27] Again, the writer uses phraseology which the Old Testament helps us to understand. For Moses had once said to all Israel, *Beware lest there be among you a man or woman or family or tribe, whose heart turns away this day from the* LORD *our God to go and serve the gods of those nations, lest there be among you a root bearing poisonous and bitter fruit*.[28] What is feared, therefore, is lest one of their number, one of those who profess faith in Christ, should turn away and become apostate. This is at once seen to be the more serious because, if it happens, it must cause spiritual damage to the whole community and involve *"the many"* in defilement.

Nor is this a peril which no longer besets God's people. Are there not in our day not only individual members, but even ministers and teachers of the Christian Church, who sometimes express great hesitation about accepting some fundamental Christian doctrines, and who even take the step of openly repudiating some divinely revealed truths? Are we as aware as we ought to be of the damage and defilement which they cause to the Church as a whole?

Thirdly, there is the peril lest any one become *immoral or irreligious like Esau, who sold his birthright for a single meal*.[29] Again we need to turn to the Old Testament fully to appreciate the force

---

[24] I Ki. 18:21.   [25] 12:15.   [26] Cf. 4:1.
[27] 12:15.   [28] Deut. 29:18.   [29] 12:16.

of this warning.[30] By birth and upbringing Esau enjoyed great spiritual privileges. But he had no proper reverence and regard for the things of God. He was entirely sensual, a man for whom nothing was sacred; a man who, when decisive choice had to be made, preferred immediate passing fleshly gratification to permanent God-given enrichment. Also, as his story tragically shows, once such a choice was made and acted on, there was no going back on it. It could not be undone. Its consequences could not be reversed. The blessing which might have been his was lost for ever.

No wonder, therefore, that this writer is so eager to awaken his readers to their personal and corporate responsibility to take care lest these dangers overtake them. They ought, he says, all to be on the watch, or "looking carefully"[31] lest any one of their number fail or fall short. The word used here for "seeing to it" expresses the idea of exercising oversight. It is in the Greek the root which gives us our word "episcopacy". Here significantly the episcopacy enjoined is not that of the one over the many but of the many over the one.[32]

What we are here exhorted to do is as Christians to help one another to sustain our faith and devotion. We ought to treat the care of the individual in need or danger as the responsibility of the fellowship. For the faint-hearted and despondent often cannot help themselves. They need the help of understanding sympathy and brotherly encouragement. So, for instance, Eliphaz said to Job, *"Behold, you have instructed many, and you have strengthened the weak hands. Your words have upheld him who was stumbling, and you have made firm the feeble knees."*[33] This is an example to be followed. So Isaiah says, *Strengthen the weak hands, and make firm the feeble knees. Say to those of a fearful heart, "Be strong, fear not!"*[34]

Also, the best remedy against such perils as are here in mind is positive not negative. As Christians we ought to live with less half-heartedness and with more consistency and straightforwardness than many of us do. We ought clearly to identify life's priorities – the ends in life that matter most; that is, not only *peace with all men*, but also that "holiness" or *consecration* which is an indispensable qualification for fellowship with God. These priorities should

---

[30] See Gen. 25:28–34; 27:1–39.   [31] 12:15, RV.
[32] Cf. 3:12, 13; 4:1; Gal. 6:1.   [33] Job 4:3, 4.
[34] Isa. 35:3, 4. Heb. 12:12 may be understood as having this sense.

then be made the object of our ceaseless quest. For peace and holiness can be possessed and enjoyed only if they are continually sought after. We should always be hot in their pursuit.[35]

Privileges to be Embraced: 12:18-24

These verses give us a crowning declaration of the blessings which become ours in Christ and under the new covenant. The writer here makes a final effort to help his readers to appreciate the wealth of their inheritance in Christ in order to persuade them to hold fast their hope steadfast unto the end. Who could think of drawing back when such blessings are already ours and are simply waiting to be possessed?

The glory and wonder of these blessings are thrown into strong relief by contrast with the features characteristic of the inauguration of the old covenant at Sinai. There what happened was terrifying and forbidding. The place was overshadowed by cloud and darkness, storm and fire. The people could not endure to hear what was spoken. God appeared awful and unapproachable.

How different the heavenly Zion to which we have come! Everything here is both glorious and welcoming – not terrifying and forbidding. God is revealed as still the judge of all, yet gracious and bountiful. Here there is full freedom of access. What is more, in Christ realized enjoyment is, or ought to be, already ours. For the writer here no longer says, "*let us draw near*",[36] but "*you have come to Mount Zion*". The experience of all who do is one not of forbidding fear but of welcoming festivity. The angels, who at the theophany at Sinai added to the awe, here express overflowing joy[37] and encourage the redeemed to share in it.

All who thus come to Mount Zion become privileged sharers in a heavenly inheritance. They become aware that they belong by grace to a select company or "assembly and church of the first-born who are enrolled in heaven".[38] Here, too, they are confirmed in faith's conviction concerning ultimate heavenly reward and fulfilment. For here are *the spirits of just men made perfect*.[39] The men of faith of Old Testament times are thus seen to enjoy now in Christ a perfection unattainable before His redeeming work was accomplished.

[35] 12:14.
[36] 10:22; cf. 4:16.
[37] Cf. Lk. 15:7, 10.
[38] 12:23, RV.
[39] 12:23; cf. 11:40.

H

Finally, as the centre and crown and cause of all we are thus given to enjoy is *Jesus* Himself, whose shed and *sprinkled blood* does not cry for vengeance as the blood of Abel cried against Cain, but speaks of an accomplished peace with God for sinners such as we are. *Jesus* is, too, Himself *the mediator* or executor of the *new covenant*, fully qualified and able, and always waiting, to fulfil its promises to all who come to Him, and to God by Him.[40] So full salvation is or can be ours.

The Prospect Before Us: 12:25-29

Our God is a consuming fire.[41] The terrors of Sinai did bear witness to the awful holiness of God. *His voice then shook the earth;*[42] and that was but a sign and symbol of His right to bring the whole created order under judgment. It is, therefore, impossible, by refusing to hear His word, to escape having dealings with Him. For *he has promised, "Yet once more I will shake not only the earth but also the heaven".*[43] Then, as Christ anticipated in His teaching, *heaven and earth will pass away.*[44] The transient is thus to disappear; the abiding and the eternal will survive and stand openly revealed. For the things which cannot be shaken will remain.[45]

It is for us, therefore, to seek to be ready for that day by heeding God's word which He is now speaking, and which cannot similarly pass away; and by putting our confidence not in vainly fancied earthly security but in the things of God which cannot be shaken. For *Jesus Christ,* our God-given Saviour, *is the same yesterday and today and forever.*[46] In and through Him we receive for our present and unending enjoyment *a kingdom that cannot be shaken.*[47]

An Appeal for Full Response

Before such a word from God the one thing not to do is to refuse to respond. So *see that you do not refuse him who is speaking.*[48] The writer here doubtless had in mind words of warning spoken by Moses. Before his death he had said to the Israelites, *Take heed to yourselves lest you forget the covenant of the LORD your God, which he made with you. . . . For the LORD your God is a devouring*

---

[40] 12:24.   [41] 12:29.   [42] 12:26.
[43] 12:26; See Hag. 2:6, 21.   [44] Mk. 13:31; cf. Rev. 21:1.   [45] 12:27.
[46] 13:8.   [47] 12:28; cf. Dan. 2:24; 7:18, 27.   [48] 12:25.

fire, a jealous God.[49] Moses was thus God's messenger who warned on earth. But now in Christ God has spoken in person Himself from heaven; and His voice abides. He is speaking still. So our responsibility to answer is not lessened but increased by hearing the gospel. Much less than the Israelites shall we escape punishment if we disobey. Much more ought we to respond in willing obedience.

Therefore let us be grateful for receiving a kingdom that cannot be shaken, and thus let us offer to God acceptable worship, with reverence and awe.[50] The older versions render "receiving a kingdom . . . let us have grace whereby we may offer service". Our response should be both to appropriate "grace" and express "gratitude". For God-given grace is our sole and necessary equipment to render acceptable service; and unceasing gratitude should be the motive force of our devotion. As priestly worshippers granted full access to the sanctuary of God's presence we ought therefore to offer to Him ourselves and the daily obedience of our lives. This should, too, always be done *with reverence and awe,* without presumption or contemptuous familiarity, remembering that *our God* – the God whom by grace we thus know in Christ, and can call our own – is a God of uncompromising holiness, *a consuming fire.*[51] This fire, which will in God's day of judgment work destruction, is now in this the day of His grace to be trusted to work in us to burn up dross and to inflame devotion.

[49] Deut. 4:23, 24.   [50] 12:28; see AV and RV.   [51] 12:29.

Twelve

Finding Our All in the Unchanging Christ

13:1-25

CHRISTIANITY IS CHRIST. *Jesus Christ is the same yesterday and today and forever.*[1] Those who have Him have all. Therefore, *be content with what you have; for he has said, "I will never fail you nor forsake you".*[2]

Practising Love: 13:1-7, 17-19

Faith and hope find their completion in love – the active love of faith and good works.[3] Wholehearted devotion to Christ, true love for Him, will show itself, as He explicitly taught and demanded, in keeping His commandments.[4] His new commandment is in particular that as His followers and friends we should love one another.[5]

Active "brother-love" should, therefore, be a characteristic of the Christian community. So let it continue; keep up its active expression.[6] As Christians we ought, too, to love one another not as though we were brethren, but because we are brethren. "This feature of love to our fellow-Christians, simply because they are Christians, is a prominent feature of New Testament religion. It almost seems as though the very word for this brother-love, the word 'philadelphia', was coined as the result of this Christian attitude."[7]

Nor should such outgoing of love be limited to fellow-Christians whom we already know, and whose present fellowship we regularly enjoy. It should also be active in welcoming newcomers, in showing hospitality to strangers, and in remembering the absent, particularly those who are suffering imprisonment or ill-treatment for Christ's sake. Since we, too, are "in the body", we have a capacity for fellow-feeling with their pains. Nor ought we to forget that, while

[1] 13:8. [2] 13:5. [3] See 10:22-24.
[4] See Jn. 14:15, 21, 23. [5] See Jn. 13:34, 35; 15:12. [6] See 13:1.
[7] See W. H. Griffith Thomas, *"Let us go on"*, p. 183.

we are still in the body, what is their lot today may be our lot tomorrow.[8]

Similarly, love in action, love of others for Christ's sake, will express itself in a proper reverence for the marriage relationship, and in a worthy enjoyment of its sacred intimacies. Sexual intercourse thus rightly enjoyed is not sinful or defiling. But we have no freedom to engage in immoral and unlawful indulgence, and to think that, because we are Christians, we shall escape the judgment of God against such wrongdoing.[9]

True love for Christ will also find expression in a new attitude towards the things of this life. Christ Himself made it unmistakably plain that attachment to earthly riches can make impossible wholehearted attachment to Himself. We cannot serve God and mammon.[10] *"Take heed"*, Christ said, *"and beware of all covetousness"*.[11] So the writer here says, *Keep your life free from love of money, and be content with what you have.*[12] Otherwise the cares and riches and pleasures of life may choke spiritual growth and prevent us from being faithful for Him.[13]

Just as in a human family reverence for God is shown by honouring one's parents, so in the Christian family devotion to Christ is shown by a right regard for those who are over us in the Lord. First, looking back, we should remember those to whom we owe our knowledge of the things of God. As we see in their history the satisfying ends to which their devotion led, we should seek to order our lives in the same way and to *imitate their faith.*[14]

Secondly, as members of a congregation of God's people we should recognize that God has given to its leaders or ministers responsibility for its spiritual oversight. Such men will therefore have to give account to God of their care and concern for our spiritual welfare. Consequently it is for us in our own interests, as well as for their satisfaction, to give them the obedience and submission that their position deserves.[15]

The Unchanging Christ: 13 : 5, 6, 8, 9

Be content with what you have. If we look at our earthly resources this may seem impossible advice to obey. But the writer here goes

[8] See 13 : 2, 3. [9] See 13 : 4. [10] Matt. 6 : 24.
[11] Lk. 12 : 15. [12] 13 : 5. [13] See Lk. 8 : 14.
[14] 13 : 7. [15] See 13 : 17.

on to add, *for he has said, "I will never fail you nor forsake you"*.[16]
So we always have Him, and He is always enough. Indeed, He
makes us truly "content" or "self-contained"; no longer dependent
on changing circumstances or uncertain external supplies, but
upheld by His abiding presence and unfailing help. So, when we are
tempted to be despondent, when life and its demands seem too
much for us, *we can confidently say*, or triumphantly sing,

> *"The Lord is my helper,*
> *I will not be afraid;*
> *What can man do to me?"*[17]

All that Christ was to us in the yesterday of our first experience
of His saving power, He is and can be to us today, and He will be
without change for ever.[18] No wonder St. Paul wrote, *I have learned,
in whatever state I am, to be content. I can do all things in him
who strengthens me.*[19]

It is, however, just here in the sphere of personal relation to
Christ, and personal reliance upon Him only, that it is all too easy
for true Christians to *be led away by diverse and strange teachings*.[20] We can be tempted unprofitably to become "sacramental" or
"religious", to hope to get benefit from things of which we physically partake, or from rules which we observe; and to forget that
what our hearts need is to be *strengthened by grace*, that is, to be
sustained by Him. So commenting on this verse, William Barclay
has written, "It is quite likely that we have got here a reaction
against an overstressing of the sacraments."[21] On the other hand, F.
Delitzsch points out that the word here used for "foods" is a term
ordinarily used in the precepts referring to clean and unclean meats;
and that it occurs elsewhere in the New Testament in passages
which refer to what was allowed or disallowed in the matter of
food.[22] So he concludes that, "when St. Paul, writing to the Roman
church, urges that the kingdom of heaven is not food and drink, but
righteousness, peace and joy in the Holy Ghost,[23] he is saying
essentially the same thing as the apostolic writer here."[24]

[16] 13:5.
[17] 13:6.   [18] See 13:8.
[19] Phil. 4:11, 13.   [20] 13:9.
[21] *The Letter to the Hebrews*, p. 226.
[22] See Lev. 11:34; 1 Cor. 8:8; Rom. 14:15, 20.
[23] Rom. 14:17.
[24] Commentary on Hebrews, Vol. 11, pp. 381, 382.

The Demands of Full Devotion: 13:10–14

We Christians have got an altar and a sin-offering. It is to be found at the cross on Golgotha, where *Jesus suffered outside the gate in order to consecrate the people through his own blood.*[25] Those who would appropriate the benefits of His sacrifice must *go forth to him outside the camp.*[26]

Such truth provides the God-given fulfilment of the Jewish types and figures of the Old Testament. It also demands that all who would embrace its benefit must abandon the old in order to possess the new. For it is impossible – as some in the early Church were trying to be – to be half Jewish and half Christian. Doubtless, because his readers were in danger from this very peril, of Judaizing their Christianity, and ultimately failing to obtain the grace of God, the writer here indicates very emphatically the radical differences which separate the two sides, between which all must choose.

First, he points out from the details of the Jewish ritual that the priests were not permitted to eat from sacrifices offered as sin-offerings. On the great day of atonement when the sacrifice for the sin of the people was offered, and when the high priest took the shed blood into the sanctuary, the bodies of the animals slain were burned outside the camp.[27] There was no feast upon the victim as at the Passover.

On the one hand, in order to oppose misleading sacramentalism, this strong statement may be intended to indicate from the foreshadowing of the Old Testament that Christian worshippers, who as priests serve in the true tabernacle, are not meant *literally* to feed upon the body and blood of their sacrificed Saviour. Or, on the other hand, in strong contrast to Judaism, it may be asserting by implication that Christians have a new privilege not granted to the priests under the old order. For we can *spiritually* partake of our sin-offering, and appropriate by faith the benefits of Christ's passion, as often as, in remembrance of Him, we eat the bread and drink the cup of the Lord's Supper.

It certainly is this radical difference between the old order and the new which the writer next emphasizes. For the Jews of the earthly Jerusalem rejected Jesus and His claim to be the promised Christ. In their eyes He died under the curse of heaven hanging on a

[25] 13:12.　　　　　[26] 13:13.
[27] See 13:11; cf. Exod. 29:14.

tree, and so rightly outside their "holy city". To them the cross was an offence. No one born a Jew, as readers of this epistle had been, could therefore acknowledge Jesus as the Christ without making a very costly decision. In order to side with Christ and to shelter under His cross, he must be prepared to *go forth to him outside the camp*; that is, cease to be reckoned a Jew, become a virtual outsider and outcast in relation to the Jewish community, and be willing to bear abuse for Christ's sake. Also, by faith he had to begin to reckon that God's promises of a city are to find their fulfilment not in the earthly Jerusalem of this present world order, but in the heavenly city of the age to come.

Nor, if we wish to devote ourselves to Christ, can any of us escape facing similar decisive and costly choice. There is no other way fully to enjoy the benefits of His one sacrifice for sins. Christ is still rejected and despised by the many. To regard the cross of Christ as a sin-offering making possible our peace with God is still to the worldly-wise foolish and to the religiously devout an offence. There are still occasions when those who would be faithful to Christ must be willing for His sake to suffer insult and reproach as one of a despised minority. There are still occasions when they must be ready to choose rightly between clinging for salvation to an earthly and ecclesiastical institution in the vain hope that it will abide, or anticipating and appropriating by faith the coming heavenly city and the security afforded by the things which cannot be shaken.

Finding Our All in Him: 13 : 12–16, 20, 21

Christianity is Christ. We have all in Him. We may confidently hope to reach the goal of full maturity and perfection wholly and solely through Him. Therefore our song cannot but be – to Him be the glory for ever.

Christian worship needs no earthly holy city like Jerusalem or Rome as its centre. It needs no special visible temple or sanctuary, no priestly caste to mediate between God and the people. For Christ is our all in all. He is our meeting-place. Christians come together and find themselves united, not within the containing framework of an earthly institution, but by going forth to Him. They become one flock by their common relation to the one Shepherd.[28]

Christ is virtually our altar, and certainly our mediator and high

[28] See Jn. 10:16.

priest. It is through Him that we may all alike draw near to the very throne of God and share in the priestly privilege of offering sacrifice. Nor is there need any longer for sin offering to be made because through Him and His one sacrifice, *by the blood of the eternal covenant*,[29] our sins and iniquities are forgiven and forgotten. And *where there is forgiveness of these, there is no longer any offering for sin*.[30] What we may offer, and should offer without ceasing, is the *sacrifice of praise to God*.[31] In worship and prayer we call upon His name, acknowledging with our lips in wonder and gratitude both who He is and all that he has done.

What by His grace we may also now offer as acceptable to God through Jesus Christ is ministries of practical kindness to our fellowmen, particularly our Christian brethren. So, says this writer here, *do not neglect to do good and to share what you have, for such sacrifices are pleasing to God*.[32]

Now may the God of peace . . . equip you with everything good that you may do his will, working in you that which is pleasing in his sight.[33] Here we have the writer's final prayer for his readers. He desires for them nothing less than their full participation in God-given life and in acceptable service. He looks to God first to work in them, to rectify what may be wrong, to supply what is lacking, that in character and conduct they may be essentially good and pleasing to God. Then he asks that, being thus qualified for service, they may be used as God's fellow-workers, to do His will. Could more or better be desired? Have we any spiritual ambitions of this sort? Is this the kind of prayer we pray either for ourselves or for our fellow-Christians?

Nor is such praying mere pious wishful dreaming of what can never be. For God has pledged Himself in covenant thus to work in us. The covenant has been ratified by the shed blood of Christ. The covenant thus established is eternal. God will never cease to operate it for our benefit.

Nor is that all. God has also *brought again from the dead our Lord Jesus, the great shepherd of the sheep*.[34] Here is the one significant mention in this epistle of Christ's resurrection. What is here emphasized is that God raised Him not simply on His own account and for His own benefit, but as *our Lord Jesus*, and as *the great shepherd of the sheep*. Such an act of God is proof and guarantee

[29] 13:20.   [30] 10:18.   [31] 10:15.
[32] 10:16; cf. 1 Pet. 2:5.   [33] 13:20, 21.   [34] 13:20.

that He means us all who are Christ's to enjoy the benefits which
He died to procure for us. So "heirs of salvation"[35] is no empty title.
Full salvation is and can be ours; and

all

through Jesus Christ;

to whom be the glory for ever and ever.

Amen.[36]

[35] 1:14 AV.
[36] 13:21.

Indexes

GENERAL INDEX

INDEX OF SCRIPTURE PASSAGES
quoted or referred to, other than those from
the Epistle to the Hebrews